Sometimes Courage

Kitty Robinson

DEDICATION

This book is dedicated to those who see the mountain looming ahead of them and wonder how they'll ever have the strength to climb it. The courage will come... one step at a time.

CONTENTS

Introduction

I walked into our large bathroom, still sweaty from my morning run. Strands of my hair that had worked their way out of my ponytail hung around my flushed face. The neckline of my workout tank was low enough to reveal the first couple inches of my open-heart surgery scar. Casey, having just finished up a shower, was standing at the sink wrapped in a towel and brushing his teeth. Looking up at the mirror he was facing, he saw my reflection breezing through the doorway. He rinsed out his mouth and smiled his dimpled smile at me through the mirror before turning to give me a good morning kiss. He aimed his lips for my forehead and put his right hand on the back on my neck. After giving my head a tender peck, he left his hand on my neck and began to feel around through my hairline. "There it is," he said as his pointer finger settled on the end of a long scar that ran from the base of my skull up to the crown of my head. "I forget that's there sometimes," he admitted. "Hard to believe we went through all of that together."

"Yeah," I agreed, "it feels like a lifetime ago..."

No one ever saw my brain surgery scar and my heart surgery scar only showed depending on what shirt I put on. Yet both scars hold tales that beg to be told. The story starts on a dirt road on the edge of a small Florida cow town. I started my running career as a barefooted girl on that dirt road. Our house was no more than 900 square feet, which was shared by four of us: my dad, my brother, Chad, my grandmother, and me.

My parents divorced when I was just four. After the divorce, I was raised by my father, who was awarded custody of my brother and I while my mom remarried, had a baby, and retained custody of my two older sisters. When people asked how a single dad got custody of his young daughter, I never had an answer.

I just know that I lived with dirt on my face and with more under my nails. My brother, Chad, and I loved being outside with the neighbor kids. Sometimes our fun was having an innocent game of football in the front yard, and other times we may have been trespassing in our crazy neighbor's orange grove. But we were always on the move and challenging each other with crazy shenanigans. Chad and I grew up racing from mailbox to mailbox. He always won but that didn't keep me from trying to beat him again and again. We loved sprinting to the cemetery that was at the end of the road, clambering to our favorite trees to climb or hustling home when dad whistled us in for the night. My life in those early years was always full of skinned knees and heart-racing adventures.

I had no idea that when I finally grew out of pigtails, tomboy bumps, and bruises, I would face surgeries that would leave me with scars that would never fade. These were scars that weren't the result of my activity but rather a sign of the Lord's faithfulness in saving my life... more than once. I had no idea that

I would stand at the starting line of the Boston Marathon the year of the bombing and, exactly one year later, pull through an emergency heart surgery just in the nick of time. As a little tow-headed country girl, I didn't know that I would birth seven children and nearly bleed out while miscarrying my eighth. I was carefree and loving life with just enough courage to climb to the tip-top of the old pine tree that lined the dirt driveway so I could announce to my big brother that from up there I could see a park, six blocks away. I had the courage to play tackle football in the rain with my older brother and all his rough and tough older friends. But I didn't have the courage to face all of the difficulties and scars that life would throw my way in just a couple of decades.

One thing that little runner-girl-turned-survivor-and-mom-of-eight has learned is that she didn't need the courage for all of the trials of life way back then. She just needed enough strength for the hours that were directly in front of her because most of the time, courage doesn't come in big doses- one year or one month or even one trial at a time- sometimes courage comes just one step at a time.

1

Young Courage

By the time I was ready to start kindergarten in 1981, Daddy, Chad, and I were settled into our tiny home while my mom, step-dad and sisters lived four hours south of us. The living conditions in the two houses couldn't have been more different. My mom and step-father, Rod, ran a furniture business together and, to a little girl growing up in an orange grove, they seemed to have everything money could buy. They lived in a modern townhouse in a gated community with swimming pools, tennis courts, a fitness center and a guardhouse. When I visited them every couple of months and for extended stays during summer breaks, I was enamored by the whole experience: from being picked up in either one of two new Toyota Camrys to sleeping in a two-story townhouse with central heat and air. Their south Florida life felt so luxurious to me.

When I went on vacations as a child, it was always with my mom and Rod. There were summers that we spent travelling cross-country in a rented RV. My mom, step-dad, four siblings and I would pile up in the camper and spend a month on the road visiting all the major landmarks out West. We stood in awe at the Grand Canyon, my little sister Vanessa skinned her knee at Mount Rushmore, and I threw a fit, refusing to take another step in the Redwood Forest. My oldest sister, Beth, and I even had the nerve to give Rod a hard time about having to stop our card game to get out of the RV to see the Badlands! We went knee boarding on the Great Salt Lake and stayed at the impressive Old Faithful Inn when our RV broke down in Yellowstone National Park.

Looking back now, I realized that while Mom and Rod were comfortable, they weren't living the highlife. They were a hardworking, middle class family who made sure their children worked hard too, but in comparison to the way my brother and I were growing up, they might as well have been millionaires.

Dad, Chad, and I lived in an old house built right in the middle of an orange grove. Our one-acre piece of property boasted amenities like good climbing trees and a dilapidated dog kennel that made a great hideout. There were orange trees everywhere with juicy fruit bending the branches and enough rotten fruit on the ground to give us kids an abundance of ammunition for some nasty orange fights.

My dad worked long hours. My aunt, grandmother, and great-grandmother lived two blocks away from us, so my brother and I often ran to their houses from the bus stop, spending a lot of our out-of-school time with them. Too many late nights of our work-weary Daddy carrying the two of us out of the beds at my grandmother's and driving us home began to wear all of us down. It wasn't long before our grandma selflessly decided to move in with us to help my dad raise us and to ensure that we would be tucked into our own beds at night.

Mema, as we came to call her, was given one of the two bedrooms in our house. I got the other bedroom and my brother used our front porch as his room. The dark and damp front porch was closed in with jalousie windows on three sides and hardwood paneling on the fourth wall, which shared a window with my grandmother's room. The porch had thick, heavy curtains all the way around and green, shaggy carpet that looked so much like grass that when a leak in the roof watered bird seed that had fallen into the carpet and sprouted, we hardly even noticed. My dad once found a snake coiled up under a pile of clothes in that carpet so apparently, we weren't the only ones who thought it looked like grass.

My dad slept in the living room most of the time- on the floor or in his recliner- wherever he landed for the night. His dresser doubled as our TV stand, but he never seemed to mind. He always sacrificed his own comfort to make sure that my brother and I had what we needed. At dinner time, we unfolded TV trays because we didn't have room for a dinner table.

When Dad was at work and Mema was gone with my aunts, my brother and I had little supervision. Along with neighbor kids, we spent a lot of time playing in the cemetery that was at the end of our road. I gave speeches to imaginary audiences from a brick stage that was used for special ceremonies and took it upon myself at times to clean the gravestones that were getting overgrown with moss. I was especially drawn to the grave markers that were in remembrance of babies put to rest there. My brother and I had also memorized the locations of the oldest people buried there and we guessed who was married to whom and knew which families were buried in groups. While other kids played the game "Ghosts in the Graveyard" in their front yards, we played it in an actual graveyard! When friends had to pass the graveyard to bring us home, we often heard comments about how creepy it must be to live by a graveyard. We never found it odd to live there and, in contrast, every time we rounded the corner to turn onto our dusty, dirt road, passing the graveyard, Daddy proudly shared his best graveyard jokes as if we had never heard them before. "Why do they put a fence around the graveyard?" he would ask, pausing to give us time to come up with an answer as if we hadn't already memorized it. "Because people are just dying to get in!" he'd bellow and then roar with laughter. We lived by a cemetery... drove old clunker cars... our house was small... but there was always room for laughter with Daddy.

Daddy had a way of making us laugh, even in difficult situations. He was always ready with a "punny" joke and a light-hearted twist on everything. This ability to find the fun and joy in even challenging situations would become a major source of support in my own life. Through his example, I learned to do the same and the trials that would come my way- from handling 3 babies in diapers at once to recovering from brain surgery- were much more bearable with a dose of laughter on the side.

When my two older sisters came to visit over the summers, we often wanted to go to town to buy snacks from the convenience store. Our only problem was that we rarely had any money. To overcome that deficit, we would gather trinkets and treasures from around the house and put them out on tables in the front yard to make impromptu yard sales. Our standards for finding items to sell weren't high. It didn't even matter to us if the stuff we chose belonged to Mema or Dad. As long as we thought it might bring in a quarter or two and wouldn't be missed, it was on the table. While some of us were setting up tables, others were hanging hand-written yard sale signs on the telephone poles on each end of the street and, in no more than an hour, our mid-week yard sale was on. The sale would stay open until we made enough money for each of us to get a drink and a candy bar, which was never more than $10. Then the tables were carried back inside, signs were torn down to eliminate the evidence and the unsold items were returned to their exact positions in the house. Before it was even lunch time we had planned, executed, and packed up a yard sale and were on our bikes to race to the convenience store in town. With two miles covered in a flash, even on our rusty, pieced-together bikes (which usually did not have enough air in the tires) we dumped our change on the store counter. We were home long before Daddy and Mema, with our bikes put away and chocolate wiped off our faces, hoping that they wouldn't find out that our front yard had been turned into a yard sale just a few hours earlier.

When I was still in elementary school, a couple that Dad was friends with encouraged him to start me in beauty pageants. Somehow my dad found a way to afford the time and cost involved to get me started in the competitions. I wore borrowed dresses until Daddy had a friend of his make one for me. Doing pageants was a way for my dad and I to spent time together, making heart connections. There were many evenings in our tiny living room where dad would coach me on turns and poise from his recliner. I practiced my pageant introductions over and over until they were perfect. I didn't practice hard because Daddy drove me hard but because it was something we were in together, so I did it for us. We were quite the pair showing up at those events- a tomboyish girl and her single dad. We never did fit in at all with the prissy girls and overbearing stage mothers. My dad would help me make sure I had everything I needed for the competitions but then could only take me as far as the door to the dressing area. As moms hovered over their daughters until the very moment they were called on stage, my dad had to sit nervously in the audience while I fended for myself backstage. At our local rodeo pageant, my daddy dropped me off at the backstage dressing room and as soon as the door shut behind me, a group of moms swarmed me- coming at me from all angles with curling irons and make-up brushes. I was in fifth grade and had basically brushed my hair and put on my cowgirl outfit, considering myself pageant ready. Surprisingly, those mamas didn't get me all dolled up, making me look 10 years older than I was. Instead, they gave me the same loving attention they gave their own girls. I don't know if they felt bad for me or they were just trying to help fill in the gaps for my daddy, who despite sacrificing in every way he could, just wasn't able to do his little girl's hair and make-up. Either way, I was show-ready in no time, with golden curls and just enough make-up to stand out.

An outsider looking in could one day see me swaying at the top of a tree and another day, playing in the mud in the driveway. But every so often, they could catch me all cleaned up, walking into our paint-chipped house in an evening gown, wearing a crown and sash and carrying a big trophy with a very proud daddy following right behind. I was 80% muddy tomboy, 20% beauty queen and 100% Daddy's Girl.

Through those pageant experiences, my dad taught me how to work hard for a goal and to accept defeat if someone else had worked harder. My blue-collar dad, who had no previous pageant exposure, taught his little girl poise, stage presence, public speaking and grace. He made me feel like I could try anything, could become good at most things and laugh at myself when I just plain failed. He did all of this with great intentionality but what he didn't know was that I was learning how much he truly sacrificed for me.

Not only did my daddy sacrifice his own comfort for us, I never once heard him complain about our living conditions. This set a great example for Chad and me. However, Chad and I were very aware of our poverty and as we grew older, we were sometimes embarrassed by it. Once, when two of my brother's high school friends came to the front door (which doubled as the door to my brother's room) Chad overheard them sneering about the condition our home was in. This was a devastating blow to him that he carried with him a long time. As an adult, Chad ended up buying our childhood home and fixing it up for his young family to live in. It was a dream come true for Chad and I to see our home, still filled with love, become a place we could both be proud of.

Our embarrassment only grew worse when Daddy had to drop us off at school or other activities because our cars were always falling apart, quite literally. One car didn't have air conditioning and in Central Florida, this meant driving with the windows down. This wouldn't have been a big deal if our car's headliner hadn't been held up with thumb tacks. When we would drive fast on highways, the wind would blow so hard that the headliner would start billowing, tossing tacks all around the car's interior. In Dad's light-hearted way, he joked that when he sold the car, he could get whatever it was worth, plus "tacks"!

When I was in middle school, my sociology class was having a party, and everyone was supposed to bring some food to share. I signed up to bring watermelon and asked my grandmother to buy one. It never occurred to me that I should bring it to class cut up and in a container. The morning of the party, I was running late for the bus (which wasn't unusual), so I snatched up that watermelon- the whole, round thing- and sprinted towards the bus. To get to the bus stop, I had to go about a tenth of a mile to the end of the road, turn left, and then run two-tenths of a mile to the bus stop. When I turned the corner, I saw that the bus had already picked up the kids from the stop and was about to pull away. I yelled for Mrs. Cramer, the bus driver, to wait and was relieved when I heard the brakes. As I ran on towards the waiting bus, the watermelon slipped from my arms, hitting the pavement. I ran after it as it rolled away from me, splitting down the middle as it went. All of this was happening as a bus full of kids looked on, laughing at me. I finally scooped up the watermelon and made it to the bus-out of breath and a bit embarrassed. But I had learned from my dad that it was alright to laugh at myself and so as I took the three steps up onto the bus and turned to face all of the kids laughing at me, I just laughed right along with them. Learning Daddy's way of being able to laugh at myself was a sure-fire bully deterrent and became one of my first lessons in courage. Having a name like Kitty, getting dropped off at school in old cars and wearing hand-me-down clothes, I could have been an easy target for bullying. When kids made a joke about me, instead of letting it hurt me, I just shot a self-directed joke back and with that, they decided I wasn't much fun to pick on and usually became a friend instead.

Dad's laughter and outgoing personality rubbed off on me enough that I was always staying after school to be part of some activity, so I rarely took the bus home. I often made the 2-mile trip home on foot. Sometimes I walked but sometimes I ran. Bookbag bouncing up and down on my back, jeans rubbing together with each stride and lace-up boots squeaking as I stepped, I probably didn't look much like a runner. But I always felt like one. Whether I was racing barefoot from mailbox to mailbox on our driveway, chasing a runaway watermelon or running home from school in worn-out boots, I *always* felt like a runner.

Despite lacking in material wealth, I never felt a lack of joy or love in our home. Mema was always singing songs of praise and regularly reminded us that this was the day the Lord had made, and we should rejoice and be glad in it! She sent us off to school with the cheerful benedictions to "Have a blessed day!" and "Be a blessing today!" and often handed us brown bag lunches with a handwritten note from either her or Daddy tucked inside. She lovingly wrote our names on the outside of our lunch bags and always added her signature smiley face under each name. Many mornings you could find the four of us holding hands in a circle in the kitchen, praying over our day before we headed out the door. We were too poor to have a dining room table but were rich enough to call on our Heavenly Father to bless and protect each of us and our teachers and our bus drivers and the lunch ladies. I don't know if there were two kids ever sent off to school under so much prayer covering.

It was in my high school P.E. class that one of the coaches encouraged me to go out for the cross-country team. Most of the students in the required class walked slowly around the track looking as if they were being asked to walk the plank by a one-eyed pirate. Meanwhile, I challenged myself to see how many laps I could do in the time allotted, all with a smile on my face. Surprisingly, I hadn't even considered joining track or cross country until Coach Robert Lindsey encouraged me to give it a try. I eagerly joined the team and felt like I had found what I was made to do. It would be just over two decades later before I would learn that the mechanics of my heart and my desire to run were on a collision course with each other.

2

Clowning, Chiari & Courage

I spent much of my high school years running track and cross country and spent the offseason warming the bench of the girls' basketball team. I was active in clubs and was the senior class president. In my senior year, our cross-country team made it to the state meet, my schoolmates voted me Miss St. Cloud High School and homecoming queen. I graduated in 1994 in the top ten percent of my class and went to a local college on scholarships. One year after graduation, I married Casey, my high school sweetheart. That poor, little country girl had grown up and life was treating her well.

Two years after we married, Casey and I were enjoying our first home, which we had renovated, and we were excitedly awaiting the birth of our first child, Kelsi May. I continued to run during my pregnancy with Kelsi, despite negative comments from family, friends, and random strangers who saw me running by as they sat on park benches. With my doctor's approval, I followed a set of rules for running while pregnant that he and I agreed on: I would never push myself to the point of breathlessness on a run (meaning no speed work or trying to beat out my big brother at the end of a run), I would always stop if I felt any form of a cramp, and I only ran the distances during pregnancy that I was running before I conceived.

Two years after Kelsi was born, unharmed from all that bouncing, the Lord blessed us with our first son, Gunner. On the morning of the day that I went into labor with Gunner, which was several days after his due date, my running partner and best friend, Celia, came to pick me up for our early morning run. When she got to the door, I told her that I had to cancel on her because I was pretty sure I was going to have a baby that day. I didn't technically have him *that* day, but since he was born in the wee hours of the next morning, I'd say my guess was pretty close.

It wasn't long after Gunner's birth that I found out I was pregnant with our third child. I continued to run during that pregnancy as well but had started wearing thick compression hose anytime I was upright to help me with the varicose veins that three back-to-back pregnancies had brought on. Those hose were so thick that even though they were nude colored, wearing them made me feel like I was wearing much more than just see-through panty hose. One morning during my pregnancy, I reached for my hose before my feet hit the floor, which was my common practice. Then I squeezed my legs into the extreme compression and headed to the closet to get dressed. I put on a t-shirt and then my socks and shoes before heading out the door. I walked outside, got into my car and began the two-mile drive to the city lakefront, where I was supposed to meet Celia for a pre-sunrise run. It wasn't until I was about to get out of the car at the lake that I realized I had never put on my running shorts. I was only wearing the nude panty hose, a t-shirt, socks and shoes!

Just a couple of months later, while on a 4-mile run with Celia and our adventurous friend, Milinda, my pace started to fall back. Like good friends do to a woman who is running while very pregnant, those two started heckling me about running so slow. By the time I got home from that run, I was in active labor and had Elizabeth Joy ("Libby") the next morning. I showed them not to tease the slow, pregnant lady!

Another sweet daughter, Annie, came a year and a half after Libby. Just before Annie's birth, Casey and I bought a new camcorder to record the sweet family times that come after the birth of a child. With my belly swollen to full term size, Casey got out the video recorder to make sure he knew how to use it before we packed it into our hospital bags. Kelsi, Gunner, and Libby were all asleep and it was just Casey and I in the living room. Casey was seated at our dinner table fiddling around with our new gadget while I stood in front of him wearing just underwear and one of his large t-shirts draped over my huge stomach. He figured out how to record and then put the camera on me. I turned away from him, with just my backside facing him and playfully lifted my shirt to show my pregnancy grannie panties. Then I joked around, asking him if I looked pregnant from the back. When I turned sideways, with his shirt pulled up to reveal my gigantic stomach, he laughed so hard at my silly antics that the camera shook in his hands as he attempted to record. I laughed too and then waddled over to him to make sure we successfully erased the video clip before we safely tucked the camera away into our bag.

When the day came for Annie to make her debut, my lifelong friend, Jessica, faithfully recorded the excitement surrounding the birth. A few weeks after welcoming Annie to the family, Casey and I took the children over to his sister Tammy's house to hang out with the family. Tammy and her husband, Bill, had a big screen TV and with Tammy, Bill, my in-laws, Casey's grandmother and his uncle all surrounding the huge television, we proudly popped in the video we had recorded of the kids meeting their new sister at the hospital. When the image began to play, there I was, to my extreme horror, on the larger-than-life screen, standing in my living room in Casey's t-shirt and underwear, showing off my full-term belly (and backside) for all to see! We obviously needed more practice with the camcorder.

Just under two years after Annie's otherwise uneventful birth, we welcomed Josie, our fifth baby in seven years. In between having Kelsi and Gunner, I had graduated from clown college.

Yes, clown college.

This "degree" had empowered me to become... a professional clown. This side job finally gave me an acceptable way to use the humor that had been passed down to me and get paid for it too! By the time we were expecting Josie, I was clowning once midweek and pretty much every weekend. Casey drove a brown Dodge Ram Charger with oversized mud tires at that time, which I occasionally had to drive to my Wednesday night clown gig. One Thursday morning, some friends of ours stopped by to tell me they had seen me the night before getting into Casey's man-toy-on-wheels. I asked where they were when they saw me and why they didn't say hello. It turned out that as they were stopped at a filling station to get gas, they looked over to the next parking lot to see a very pregnant clown struggling to get her big red shoes up onto the running boards and hoist herself into the Ram truck. They said that by the time I had made it, 9 months pregnant and wearing a red wig, into the driver's seat, they were laughing so hard they couldn't have talked to me if they wanted to. On a Wednesday night just a couple of weeks later, while painting the last few children's faces who had lined up to see "Bananas D. Clown", I went into labor with Josie. Casey was on board with the whole clowning thing, but he was insistent that he would never take a pregnant clown to the hospital to deliver a baby. Knowing

that labor was starting, I was eager to get home and make sure that
I could get out of my clown costume and makeup before we
headed to the hospital. I teased Casey with the possibility of going
to the delivery room as a clown just to get him worked up, but I
was just as against the idea as he was! We made it to the hospital
in time to deliver Josie in the triage, walking in looking like a
normal couple expecting a baby any moment. But if anyone had
looked closely, they would have seen the thin white strips of face
paint still running along the length of my eyelids.

Besides some minor wardrobe malfunctions and almost
having to check into the hospital as Bananas D. Clown, I ran
through all five of those pregnancies without issues, delivered
healthy babies and recovered quickly, returning to the sport I loved
two weeks after each birth. On the outside, I looked like the picture
of health, with or without the red nose. In those years of babies,
pregnancies, breastfeeding, toddlers, and little sleep, I appreciated
the simplicity of running and was able to stay in a consistent
groove by running in the early morning hours before the little ones
started stirring. All I had to do was surrender to the alarm clock,
lace up my running shoes and head out the door (Making sure that
I had my pants on, of course!).

Between the consistent exercise, bouncing back so well
from pregnancy, successfully breastfeeding all of my children,
running a small clowning business and delving into home
schooling the children with all my devotion, I continued to feel like
life was really going my way. At that point in parenting, I was
pretty confident that I could write a book on how to do it all and do
it all with a smile. Ever since high school I had almost come to
expect success and there it was, still flowing my way.

Just a few months after the birth of our fifth daughter, my
perfect little world came crashing down. It all started one evening

when I was getting ready for a clown job. I was painting my face to get into my character, when I turned my head to answer Casey, who was calling to me from the other room. As I turned towards his voice, I felt a strange sensation in my head that I could only describe as my head turning and my brain lagging a little behind. I mentioned it to Casey and we both agreed that maybe my blood sugar was dropping and that I probably just needed something to eat. With nursing a baby and running all those miles, I was used to some occasional dizziness related to that. However, this dizziness was noticeably different than the familiar lightheadedness that comes with needing a bite to eat. I grabbed a snack anyway and headed out the door to my clown gig.

From that day on, I began to experience more of those strange dizzy spells that came on just as unexpectedly as the first episode. One evening, I was taking a bath while my little blonde toddler, Annie, was standing at the side of the tub, splashing her hand in the water every now and then, I began to feel seasick from the movement of the water. I laughed as I described the incident to Casey but deep down, I was beginning to wonder what was happening to me. In just a couple of weeks, I went from being totally healthy to getting seasick in the bathtub. Around the same time, I also started to experience frequent heart palpitations.

Three weeks after my first episode with the dizziness, I took my kids on our weekly trip to the library but while there, I was hit with an episode that caused me to became so dizzy and disorientated that I had to feel my way along the bookshelves to get to the library office, where I could use the phone to call Casey. Just dialing his number took intense concentration. He headed our way, while I sat on the floor and leaned my head back on a bookshelf. I gathered all five children around me while we waited for Casey to come to the rescue. This was the same library that I had grown up going to as a child. That active blonde haired girl, who had once skipped down the rows of books was grown up and sitting on the floor, barely able to keep her head up. Casey made it quickly to the library and helped us all out to the car.

Sitting in the car in the library parking lot, I felt so irresponsible for getting myself and my little children stranded like that, and I felt bad that Casey had to leave work to come get us. I knew my symptoms were getting worse, but I had no idea that they could leave me unable to function. During the three weeks that had elapsed since that first dizzy spell, Casey had been encouraging me to see the doctor but, like any busy mom, I just kept putting it off. I was never one to rush to see the doctor. It wasn't something I grew up doing and avoided it as an adult, too. I did however read every article on health and wellness that I could get my hands on. No alcohol? Check. Smoking? No way. Regular exercise? Of course! Sunscreen? SPF 50. Seatbelt? Every time. I was so in control of my health that I expected the dizziness and pressure I was experiencing to go away at some point on its own. I had been doing everything right so why should there have been something wrong with me? But that day, after being unable to drive my own children home from the library on the same streets I grew up riding my bike on, I *knew* there was something wrong with me and it was obviously out of my hands. I felt so ill that I wondered if I should be in the hospital. We decided, however, to call the doctor's office and made an appointment for the following morning.

I spent the rest of the evening in bed with such severe dizziness that even just moving my jaw caused me to become nauseated. The ceiling fan whirling above my head was unbearable while any movement in my peripheral vision caused an uptick in my symptoms as well. As I laid there in bed feeling useless and tormented by dizziness, I could hear Casey putting all of the kids to bed. Soon, nights like that one began to become our new normal.

Consistent with the inconsistency of my symptoms, I woke up feeling great the next morning and struggled to explain to the doctor how bad off I was just 12 hours before. Dr. Hartman, who had been our family doctor for quite a few years, seemed to have the gift of discernment. Even though I sat in his office as the picture of youth and health that morning, after hearing my symptoms, he felt the urgency to send me for a stat MRI that day.

The actual MRI was "stat", but the results took longer than they should have. Over the course of the next week my health deteriorated so rapidly that I spent most of my time bedridden. There were halves of days that I felt OK, but once the pressure in my head began to build and the dizziness and nausea started in, my only option was to sleep it off, praying that I would wake up symptom-free the next morning. When I did feel well, I would try to cram as much life into that time frame as I possibly could to make up for the time I spent in bed.

One week after my MRI, I still had not heard back from the doctor with the results. I was becoming desperate. My day-to-day life with five children seven-and-under was physically demanding and I could no longer keep up. After reading up on vertigo, I decided that my problem must have been in my inner ear. Even though the dizziness described with inner ear issues wasn't exactly like what I was experiencing, it was the most reasonable diagnosis Google and I could come up with to explain my symptoms. I grew confident that the MRI would be fine, but I needed the doctor to confirm that so I could get a referral to an ear, nose and throat specialist. I waited a week before calling Dr. Hartman's office to try to get the results. I was feeling good enough that day to work so I made the call in the few minutes I had before I would have to begin getting ready for my weekly clown job.

When I called the doctor's office, I was routed to his nurse, who over the years, had become like a family friend. "We have the results, but it's been such a crazy week that the doctor hasn't read them yet, and he has already left for the day," she told me apologetically.

"I have gotten so much worse in this past week that I am having a hard time taking care of my own children" I replied, feeling desperate.

"I'll have him look at it tomorrow but I'm looking at it now and everything seems to be fine… just says something about Chiari Type 1 Malformation but I'm sure that's nothing of concern." I was so happy to hear her say that and felt that with a referral to the ENT from Dr. Hartman the next day, I would be on my way to getting past this unsettling time. Before we hung up, I asked her to repeat the name of the seemingly benign malformation she mentioned. With the nurse spelling C-H-I-A-R-I for me, I jotted it down on one of the kid's school papers that was piled on my desk. I had just a couple of minutes before I had to get into my "Bananas D. Clown" character so, out of curiosity, I decided to do a quick Google search on Chiari.

When typing those words into the search box on our desktop, using dial-up Internet, I had no idea what an impact the results would have on my life. Whatever condition I had, was obviously there and affecting me but *knowing* what I had changed the situation entirely in my mind. I clicked on the first reputable medical site that came up in my search only to see a picture of a surgeon and his medical staff in the operating room, encircled around a patient and performing… brain surgery. My eyes locked in on that picture and I stared in shock. *There must be some mistake.*

As I read on about Chiari (which I learned is pronounced *key-ar-ee)* and the symptoms associated with it, the feeling of a punch in the gut told me that this was no mistake. Most of what I had been feeling lined up perfectly with the symptoms I read online. My eyes darted from the list of symptoms to the picture and back to the symptoms again. *No, there has to be a mistake,* I silently pleaded as I disconnected from the dial-up connection so I could call the nurse back to clear up the dreadful confusion. *I bet she said the MRI ruled out the possibility of the Chiari Malformation. She probably said, "No Chiari Type 1 Malformation" and I misheard her.* But, like a tidal wave, the list of symptoms that I had just read online crashed over my attempt at explaining the diagnosis away. The two theories continued to clash in my mind as I dialed the doctor's office. The receptionist answered. She politely informed me that Dr. Hartman's nurse had left for the day and I would have to call back tomorrow.

"But I was just talking to her a few minutes ago. Can you see if she's in the parking lot? Or can you go look at my MRI and tell me if I do or don't have Chiari Malformation? I have to know now." My voice was desperate as I began to lose all patience and sense. Of course, she wasn't going to run out to the parking lot or go dig up my file and she politely told me just that. I hung up and my mind began to crank out ideas on how I could find out my medical fate without having to wait until the next day.

I knew where Doctor Hartman lived so I could just drive over to his house but that seemed a bit too stalkerish (I knew he wouldn't have my test results at his house anyway). After ruling out other unreasonable ideas- like putting up a billboard- I looked up his home number in the phone book and, breaking all patient/doctor protocol, left a message on his home phone. That was all I could do. As much as the dilemma rattled me, I knew I had to move on until I heard something back from the doctor. My children needed me, and I had to get ready for my clown job.

When Casey got home, I was on the phone explaining everything to my mom while simultaneously painting my face. This meant Casey walked into the house hearing second hand that I may need brain surgery. When I hung up with mom, and still in my clown getup, I filled Casey in on parts of the conversation with my mom that he missed until I was interrupted by the phone ringing. It was Doctor Hartman. He had gotten my message and driven back to his office to review my MRI report before returning my call. This was just one of the reasons we loved our dear Dr. Hartman.

"I'm sorry," he started in his comforting voice, "but you *do* have a condition called Chiari Type 1 Malformation and there's nothing I can do for you about it. You will have to see a neurosurgeon." How fitting that I would receive that news while dressed as a clown, right down to the big red shoes because I would need a hefty dose of humor to get me through the deep valley that I was about to walk through.

3

Courage to Let Go

I waited several long, trying weeks to see the neurosurgeon. During that time, I sat helplessly by, watching my life being stripped away from me because of my deteriorating health. At the same time, a new life was being handed to me. It was up to me to willingly release the old life and humbly accept the new. It was through this transfer that I would find truly abundant life.

My old life consisted of a lengthy list of accomplishments and accolades that I felt made up who I was. At 29 years old, I was building on my high school success from a decade before. I took pride in still being married to my high school sweetheart and read plenty of books on marriage to make sure that we had the best and strongest marriage possible. I wanted to honor the Lord in our marriage, but I attributed all of its success to my own efforts.

After I graduated, I never stopped running and felt that being a runner was more than just something I did, it was part of who I was. I loved it, I pushed myself at it and deep inside, I prided myself in it. Being able to run through all of my pregnancies and return to running only two weeks after each birth only further puffed me up. It also kept me from gaining too much weight during my pregnancies and took me back to my pre-pregnancy weight insanely fast, which made me feel amazing. People were always impressed with my success in this area and I ate it up.

Nine days after the birth of my fifth child, which was just a few months before my diagnosis, and already back into my pre-pregnancy clothes, I decided to join my older sister, Amy to run in a 5K put on by our local run club. I had never returned to running so quickly but I felt good enough to give it a try. Inside, I was so impressed with how great I looked that I was eager to get out and show others. Knowing that they would be astonished that I was back to running so soon motivated me even more. As I headed out the door to go to the 5K, I reassured Casey, who was questioning the whole idea, that I would mostly walk and would take it very easy. But once the run started, I couldn't help myself. Though I started at a slow pace, I saw my sister moving further away from me and I just couldn't stand it. I wanted to be up there with her. So, I began to pick up the pace, pushing myself. As I passed other runners, I was fueled by their comments about how good I looked or about how amazed they were that I had just had a baby and yet was passing them. It's hard to admit but I thrived on this type of affirmation. After the run was over, I hung around run club just long enough to hear more of the same positive comments about myself before I hurried home to nurse my nine-day old baby.

As I sat cuddled up with baby Josie, nourishing her body from mine, I felt like I could do it all- I had just run a 5K nine days after having my fifth baby! Within an hour or so though, my body began to scold me and proved to me that I was wrong. Though I had felt healed from the outside, I had overestimated the healing process that was going on inside. My insides hurt to such an extreme that I was nearly brought to tears. I began to cramp and bleed heavily. I was sure that I had undone all the healing that had been silently happening over the previous week and a half. I ached so badly but I couldn't complain because I knew I had foolishly done it to myself, all for the approval of others.

I worked to earn other people's approval in other ways, too. Home schooling was something that Casey and I believed the Lord had called us to when I was pregnant with our oldest, Kelsi. I started right away, buying a belly belt with speakers that I could hook a Walkman into. I played classical music and children's Bible songs to my unborn child and read to her daily. Two weeks after Kelsi was born, I started an extensive "Teach Your Baby to Read" program. By the time she was three, she was doing a full reading curriculum, had memorized the books of the Bible, and knew most of her state capitals. I found that I was very good at teaching her and we both enjoyed the time together. However, pride took over when I wanted her to show off to others. I recall intentionally leaving her school books out so house guests would ask about them only to learn how advanced our preschooler was. This was just another idol from which I drew my worth and identity. I continued to teach the other children as each came along. I started early in the morning, incorporating my children's educations into everything we did. I looked down on the idea of using worksheets and workbooks. Instead, I stayed up late many nights planning elaborate unit studies and making intricate activities. This method was, in my mind, the best way for children to learn, so I gave it all I had.

We've all heard that it takes a village to raise a child, and I believe in that old saying now, but before everything began to unravel, I was pretty sure that I could raise a perfect little brood of warriors for the Lord if everyone around me would just keep an arm's length away. Unless, of course, they were willing to submit to my exact methodology. This went for my husband, too. I wanted my children to eat the perfect diet, to have a balanced exposure to art, education, Christianity, music and language. The kids were to be well mannered, well spoken, and well behaved. I knew these things would be caught, not taught, so I was constantly getting on Casey for not using good manners around the children. I corrected him if he raised his voice or talked too much slang to our kids. I prided myself in the level of patience I had with the kids but couldn't show Casey grace when he wasn't as patient. I really felt that *I* was the parent who had read the books and had figured things out and that he should just follow my lead.

This level of pride I had in what I did flowed over into breastfeeding, natural childbirth, home organization and more. It wasn't that I looked down at people who didn't do these things, but I wanted them to look up at *me* for doing them. Worse than that, I had built for myself a tidy little Christian package that I just knew must have pleased my Heavenly Father. I felt His approval for me wasn't because of what Christ did for me, but instead was because of all I had to offer to his kingdom. The things I did and felt accomplished in weren't evil but the way I exalted them in my life most certainly was.

For the first couple of weeks after my Chiari diagnosis, people openly complimented how I was handling the news with humor and strength. This approval of others just fueled my actions. However, inside of me a storm was brewing. I was beginning to lose so much of the control that I thought I had over my life. I was feeling exposed. Casey was having to take on the majority of the care for the children when I wasn't feeling well, and I had to just sit back and watch him do everything the "wrong" way. I couldn't even correct him because I was often too dizzy to speak! Like the night of the episode I had at the library, I spent many nights alone in bed, staring at the ceiling, unable to do anything. I had to give up driving which meant I couldn't grocery shop for my family or take the kids to the library every week. I couldn't run anymore either. Where I had once looked down on using worksheets for my children because that wasn't up to my educational standards, I found that I didn't have the mental clarity to even go down the stairs to our school room to search through materials to pull out worksheets for the children. Being incapable of even pulling together worksheets for my kids was a new low.

One night, while laying beside Casey in our bedroom, the facade I had been holding up tumbled down and I began to weep and basically whine. "I just don't understand why this is happening to *me*. I was doing everything right and was at the top of my game. Now, I can't even brush my teeth without getting dizzy. Why, Casey? Why? These things don't happen to me. I had it all together. I was the homecoming queen!" Right about that point, Casey's work radio alerted him that he was being called out on an emergency. He looked at me with the saddest eyes and told me he had to go. Although, inside, he was probably relieved that he didn't have to sit through anymore of my whining. He left my pity party, leaving me there with no one to listen to it, making it a most pitiful pity party. Without a person in the room for me to cry to, my thoughts turned to the Lord and I began to ask Him, "Why me? Why did I have to walk this path?"

As I prayed though, I noticed a change happening in my heart. The Lord seemed to be working immediately by changing my thought patterns. With his gentle guidance I realized that my only reality was the path that was in front of me. Dwelling on the "why me" question wasn't getting me anywhere. Unless the Lord miraculously healed my congenital brain defect, I was going to have to walk that road. I had no choice. But what I could choose was *how* I would walk it. Would I whine and complain? Would I be held by fear and anxiety? Would I try to put up a false front to others? More importantly, would I continue to find my worth in the things I had done? My Father beckoned softly, what if I focused on whose child I was? What if I put my full trust in him, walking the journey in peace, joy, and hope? What if I allowed him to strip me of the self-fulfilled life I had been building this whole time? What if, he whispered, I let him rebuild my entire life around the firm foundation of Jesus Christ, His Son? Those were the only options before me and, though the answer wasn't easy, it was clear. That night, I committed my life to the Lord in a new way and gave Him complete control, having no idea what the outcome would be. This, I would learn, is what it truly means to put feet to my faith.

In the weeks leading up to my appointment with the neurosurgeon, pre-operative testing and ultimately brain surgery, I became dependent on others in a way that I would have been too prideful for before the night of my pity party. The old me would have been too proud to accept help from others but the new me was in awe of how the Lord used others to fill in the gaps in my life. The old me would have felt that other people couldn't step in and do my tasks as good as I did them but the broken me was just so thankful to have the help. I learned not only to accept help but also to ask for help when I needed it, even if I did call and hang up on a friend a few times before I got up the nerve to ask her to come take the kids for me on a particularly rough day.

When I was disappointed that I could no longer take the kids to the library, I began to pray about it. Without me saying a word to anyone about it, I received an email from one of the librarians who had heard of my diagnosis. She offered to bring books by every week and pick them up when she delivered a new batch. When I felt up to it, I could email her a list of books I wanted, and she would pick them out for us. And when I couldn't get myself together to do that, she would surprise us with her best picks. Her name was Bethia, but I called her my Library Fairy!

One afternoon I sat in my kitchen, leaning against the wall, with my head hung low, wondering how I was going to handle groceries and menu plans. I decided to give that to the Lord, too, and within minutes, the doorbell rang. When I got to the door, no one was there but there were bags of groceries on my front steps, along with a note from my friend, Jessica. The note informed me that she wanted to take over my grocery shopping until further notice.

As I racked my brain, trying to figure out how I would keep up with the kids' schooling, my friends and homeschool co-op partners, Kelly and Heidi, offered to homeschool my kids right along with their own children. They arranged with Casey when they would pick them up and bring them home so I wouldn't have to worry about the details. They also taught them in the same style I would have used, which didn't matter to me anymore by that point. but it sure was a nice perk. They took them on fun field trips and helped them have the sense of normalcy that they so desperately needed as their lives drastically changed.

I felt incredibly blessed as I witnessed people stepping in to take over so many of my responsibilities. Of course, no one could step in to run for me but that was just something I had to let go. I trusted the running would come back to me someday. But for the first time, I felt complete, even without it. In hindsight, it was clear that losing running for a season was necessary for it to have the proper place in my life. I grew thinner and I grew weaker. Over time, I watched my running muscles atrophy, but running was so far down on my list of priorities by then that it didn't bother me.

Laura was a friend from church who was known in our circle of friends for her bright mind, put together looks, and ultra-organized ways. She was also known for her kindness and giving spirit which was evident when she offered to come clean my house weekly until I had recovered. When other friends heard that I had accepted Laura's offer, they questioned my willingness to have Laura see my dirty toilets and stained carpet. She was the kind of person you would want to clean for *before* she came over to clean for you. However, I had no hesitation in saying yes to Laura's sweet gesture. I had learned that when I accepted help from others, it would bless me for sure but would bless them even more. I never knew what kind of mess Laura would show up to, but I was thankful every time she came to clean my full house.

Even though I hadn't lived in the same town as my mother since I was four years old, she always made great efforts to be present in important moments of my life whenever it was in her power to do so. She would drive up from her home in south Florida to spend a week with me after the births of each of my children. During those visits, we bonded over follow-up doctor's appointments, taking care of the other children and just sitting and staring at whoever was the newborn at the time. She put great attention into meals I was eating to make sure I was getting the quality calories I needed to heal and to provide nutrient dense breast milk to my babies. We went on light outings together and took walks that became more and more of a production to make happen as we added more children to the family, but she never seemed deterred. She also brought along a highlighting kit to highlight my hair as her little way of pampering her daughter, the new mama. When she wasn't welcoming a new grandbaby, my mom made it a priority to be at the kids' birthday parties, even though it usually meant driving four hours, celebrating with us and then getting back in the car for the four-hour trip home. Mom committed to making that same long drive during my recovery. This time however, instead of celebrating her grandchildren, she offered to tackle all of our laundry. A poor reward for a four-hour drive!

During my sickness, Mom made that same eight-hour round trip every week- just to do our laundry. True to her style, Mom established a routine with the kids, promising them that if all of their dirty clothes were in their basket when she arrived to do laundry, she would take them to Dairy Queen when the last of the freshly laundered clothes were tucked into their drawers. Mom did this for us for over two months.

Before I even had surgery, my sister-in-law, Steffanie, put together a four-month long meal train for us. She did this prior to the days of social media and meal train websites where getting people signed up is as easy as clicking "send." Somehow, she got the word out and had the calendars organized from people all over the community that covered meals for us for four months! One night, dinner was brought to us by my second-grade math teacher, who I probably hadn't seen since grade school. On some nights, dinners were brought to us by friends we hadn't seen since high school and other nights, it was brought to us by parents of friends we hadn't seen since high school. So many people from church, running club and even friends of friends wanted to sign up that Steffanie had to tell some of them to bring us breakfast instead of dinners. Our kids were so used to hearing the doorbell ring and then having our dinner walked into us, piping hot and ready to eat that before long, they expected food at the door every time they heard the doorbell.

Personally, I went from a young mom who dizzied herself by trying to look like she had it all together to someone completely dependent on others for her needs. In that transformation, I learned how to admit that I couldn't do everything, and I grew comfortable asking for help, reminding myself often that the one who *gives* receives an even bigger blessing than the one in need. I found joy in receiving care from friends instead of working so hard to look like I was the last person to need help. I experienced such freedom in this soul evolution that I felt I could soar even when confined to a bed.

Before getting sick, I was so busy doing *things* that I didn't really have much time for *people*. When I did have people over, I would stress so much about how our house looked that I sucked the joy out of the evening before our guests even arrived. After I became sick and knew that people would be in my house daily, I had no choice but to give up the high expectations I had for how our home looked. I was also having to lie down so much that when people did visit, there was nothing else to occupy me except their presence. In the mornings, I would check the calendar to see who was bringing dinner, and all day I would look forward to spending time with them. And instead of spending the time leading up to welcoming visitors frantically cleaning the house and ordering everyone around, I learned to pray for those who were coming to see me. I hoped that when they brought the food, they would sit down and stay awhile, keeping me company and letting me hear about all that was going on in their lives. While some people did spend time with me, I found that the majority of our thoughtful dinner-deliverers were too busy to enjoy a little face-to-face time. So many of them reminded me of the Tasmanian Devil, frantically spinning into our kitchen, dropping a meal on the counter and then whirling out the door before I could even sit up on the couch. They were where I had been if my crazy spinning hadn't been brought to a halt by Chiari. Without Chiari, I might never have gained the new and refreshing perspective that I felt fortunate to have discovered.

Other friends sent us cards, gift cards, and money to help with inevitable expenses related to my illness. Men from church came over one Saturday to turn part of our garage into a room for me. Our bedroom was upstairs in our two-story house and I was advised that stairs would be too difficult for me to handle during my recovery. One Saturday night after surgery, our Pastor, Bob Chambers and his thoughtful wife, Joy, came over to bathe the kids, put them in bed and set out their church clothes so we could make it to church the next morning. Casey had wanted us to go but he was carrying so much of the burden that having the Chambers (who were parents to eight children of their own) lighten the load was monumental.

At one point, I told Casey that I felt like I was living through my funeral. When he asked what I meant, I told him that most people don't know how much they're loved until it's too late. They die and then people from their past and present come out of the woodwork to attend the funeral, bring flowers, drop off food for the family and linger as they tell old, funny stories. I sometimes felt like I was on the outside looking in and had the unique perspective of seeing the kind of outpouring that people normally miss because it doesn't happen until after their death. I was loved and well cared for and I knew many of those people didn't know the pride that I carried for so long nor could they see the change that was happening inside to deliver me from that pride. But I felt it happening daily and they were all unknowing contributors to the over-due changes in my heart.

When the surgeon told us that I would need constant care for the first two months following surgery, we wondered how Casey could continue to work while I got the care I needed. My co-op friends would continue taking care of the four oldest children during most weekdays and we planned to send baby Josie to spend a week or so with Celia and her family who had moved to north Florida. After that, Josie would stay with my good friend and mentor, Denise, who lived in our neighborhood. It was devastating for me to make arrangements for my baby, who had been with me nonstop since her birth, to stay away from me. What was worse, was that the doctor firmly told me that I would not be able to nurse

Josie for at least a couple of months following surgery. I knew that this would mean my milk would dry up because breastfeeding is all about supply and demand. Secretly, I planned to find a way to get back to nursing Josie, who I thought, given my current health condition, would be my last baby. I tucked my secret plan into the back of my mind and began pumping milk to store for her and introduced her to a bottle and formula. I went from priding myself in not ever giving formula or bottles to my other babies- and even looking down on other women who did- to being so thankful that alternatives were available to keep my sweet Josie Faith alive and growing in the absence of her mother. When I did struggle with losing our nursing bond, I had to remind myself that I couldn't choose another path, but I could choose to walk the path I was on in joy and faith. It turned out that having a baby with the middle name Faith during that time was just what I needed.

With the kids' daily care figured out, we began to schedule my care. Our plan was for Casey to only work four-day weeks for eight weeks, taking off every Friday to be home with me for long weekends. Denise said she would walk over from her house on Mondays to be with me which left three days each week that still needed to be covered. My sister, Amy, who lived nearby and was working at a cleaners, chose to quit her job, committing to stay with me every Tuesday, Wednesday, and Thursday. In the past, I would have felt like an inconvenience to all of those people who were making such concessions to be there for me in my time of need. But instead, I was overwhelmed with thankfulness at their willingness to help and at God's provision for my life.

My mom, who had passed the bar exam to become an attorney the year I had Kelsi, drove up the day before surgery. She helped us put together my living will as well as other documents needed in case things went wrong in the hospital. The day before surgery, we hustled around to get papers signed and notarized.

There wasn't one ounce of fear in me as we made those preparations but she felt it was a good idea and since she had the legal means to make it happen, I obliged. It was just another way of her caring for me.

The night before surgery, I sat in the back of a church service and as the pastor was wrapping it up, he announced to the congregation that there was a young mother of five in the service who was having major surgery the next morning and that she needed prayer. My heart went out to that young woman and I started to feel sorry for her until I realized that I was the young mother he was referring to! I was so far removed from the "why me" attitude that had engulfed me weeks before that I no longer saw the desperation in my situation. I walked in perfect peace, according to the promises of God.

We were prayed over by several church members, other people at church hugged me a little tighter and a lot longer and when we got home, there were tearful messages on our answering machine from family members who were making one last call before my surgery. I quickly realized that while all of those people meant well- the hugs, the tears, the last calls, the pitiful looks- these interactions were rooted in fear and I had to guard myself from any trace of fear. Casey and I chose not to listen to the rest of the voice messages, turned off the phone and confidently headed up stairs to bed.

I slept well that night. The next morning, Casey drove me to the hospital while my mom followed close behind in her car. When I hugged them both and said goodbye before I was taken back to get prepped for surgery, I remember noticing that I felt more nervous lining up at the starting line of a 5K than I did heading into brain surgery. That could only be described as the peace of God that transcends all understanding. Our inborn human understanding tells us that we should fear the unknown, we should be scared in uncertain times and that we should crumble when stripped of who we are. But the peace of God surpasses our finite human understanding and gives us the strength to face uncertainty peacefully. It was incredible to experience something so strong and comforting that was totally apart from who I knew myself to be. I couldn't take credit for the peace that I had. On my own, I was curled up in a ball, crying "Why me?" to anyone who would listen. But with God's power working in me as I fully gave Him control, I was able to walk through one of life's most uncertain times almost as if I was in a protective bubble.

Recovering from brain surgery was hard and long. While he didn't actually cut into my brain, the doctor removed part of my skull and part of my first vertebrae. He also cut open the lining of my brain and harvested tissue from my neck to expand the lining so that my brain would have room to let the spinal fluid once again flow freely. I spent the first couple of days in ICU and woke up in a lot of pain. I don't remember a whole lot from my time in the hospital except that Casey was there with me every waking moment, tenderly seeing to my needs. He told me later that when he first saw me after surgery, he leaned in to kiss me and was immediately nauseated by a familiar smell. Unable to identify the smell, he racked his brain to find the connection. Finally, he realized that as a hunter he was used to the smell of cut bone, specifically from cutting a buck's rack from his skull. That previously unidentifiable smell he inhaled every time he kissed my forehead was the stench of cut bone and that was difficult for him to stomach.

When the doctor told me that I would be a dependent individual for two months after my surgery, what I heard him say was that I would be recovered after two months. So I was sorely disappointed when I didn't magically wake up on that 60th day feeling like my old self and being able to hold my baby again. After being away from me for several weeks, Josie, seven and a half months at that time, no longer longed to be with me and instead clung to Denise when she brought Josie over for visits. This was probably the hardest part of my recovery. When it happened the first time, I was in shock. All of my babies were clingy to me because I exclusively breastfed and was able to spend so much time with them. Before surgery, Josie had a hard time weaning from me and, at first, didn't want to have anything to do with a bottle. Now she was rejecting the very person she worked so hard to wean from. I couldn't believe my own baby was crying at being offered to me. I immediately wanted to cry at her rejection, but I felt God's timely peace assure me that it would get better with time. I soaked in that peace and resolved to work at reconnecting with Josie slowly instead of crying over the loss. In time, Josie came back to me willingly. It was still a long time before I could hold her on my own but after a lot of hard work and some dedicated help from a lactation consultant, I was even able to re-lactate and nursed Josie until her second birthday.

Over time, the Lord gave me back all that I had grieved over but as I received each treasure back, I took each one as a gift from the Lord and a tool to be used for Him instead of as something that made me honorable in His sight. I no longer desired to be admired by everyone who was looking into my life. In fact, the opposite was true: I felt naked and broken and wanted others to see how much I had to depend on the Lord for everything. My greatest fear became the thought of someone seeing a snapshot of my life and thinking, "Man, what can't she do?"

Running was probably the last gift that was returned to me. I tried running once the surgeon cleared me for activities, but every time I ran, I felt pain in the back of my head. For a time, I took up speed walking which was ironic because I once secretly jeered at speed walkers, laughing to myself at how ridiculous they looked. Pride certainly does come before a fall and once again, I found myself being thankful for the very thing I once mocked. I ended up looking forward to my mornings spent speed walking the neighborhood and didn't care that I looked just as ridiculous as the other walkers I once laughed at. I was just so happy to be able to move! It was almost a full year after my surgery before I was able to actually run, which was fine with me. I was still experiencing some heart palpitations, but my head was finally getting back to normal. While my running muscles had atrophied, my spiritual muscles had grown by leaps and bounds and though no one could see those muscles, I would have made the trade off a hundred times over.

4

Courage to Chase Dreams

I fought hard not to get sucked back into a hectic life as I recovered from brain surgery. During that time, among so many other valuable lessons, I learned that life didn't have to be so busy, always on the go. I learned to say yes to help but more than that, I learned to say no to unnecessary activities. During my recovery, I was restricted in what I could do physically, and so I gratefully cherished being home and laying on the floor playing games with my children. I no longer felt I had to struggle to be considered successful and I no longer prided myself in the praise of others. I slowed down, finding peace in my new pace and perspective.

Less than a year-and-a-half after my brain surgery, Casey and I felt a call to missions and joined the North American Mission Board as Mission Service Corps (MSC) volunteers. This was a tremendous step of faith as Casey had to quit his dependable job with good health insurance. We had to trust God to provide our monthly income through support from individuals. We both felt like the Lord had used my illness to prepare us for this next step because our values had changed so much, and our faith had grown considerably. Selling most of our belongings and leaving the security of Casey's job wasn't too hard for us because we had transferred our values into a hope for an eternal home, finding our security in Christ. In just a few months, through family and friends, the Lord had provided enough pledges for monthly support for us to move our family of seven to eastern Kentucky to begin work with a mission organization there.

For me, the hardest part of this move was leaving the community that had rallied around us during our time of need. Casey and I had both lived in the small town of St. Cloud, Florida since we were each four years old. We had deep roots there even before my health crisis. We felt so much love from so many people that leaving the comfort and familiarity of our community was heart-wrenching. The other tough part for me was knowing that I would no longer be close to my grandmother, whose health was beginning to deteriorate. She had sacrificed so much of herself to help raise my brother and me that I almost felt like a traitor for moving away. What propelled us forward though was a certainty that going on mission and moving to Kentucky was what the Lord had next for our lives. So, we walked the path in confidence, knowing who was in control.

In September of 2006, our little family from flat Florida settled in the mountainous region of Eastern Kentucky. Casey jumped right into ministry as I home schooled the kids and kept our home running. I helped with ministry when I could and found time for myself in my usual rhythm of running. Running in the mountainous coal region of Kentucky was difficult. Besides some Sunday morning "hill" workouts that my brother and I did on an overpass not far from my house in Florida, I had only run on pancake flat terrain. After some training though, my body stepped up to the challenge and adapted to the real hills on the 20-acre ministry campus that we called home. The biggest challenge for my on-campus running was the lack of variety. I found that, because of safety issues, running on campus was really my only option. The roads outside our campus snaked around steep mountain sides that lacked shoulders to step off on if an oncoming vehicle was heading my way. Most of those vehicles were large trucks carrying coal to and from local coal mines. Short roads, called hollows (pronounced "hollers"), branched off the main roads but often led to private property where unannounced visitors (or runners) weren't always welcome. Because of this, all of my running took place on less than a mile of paved roads on our campus. These roads didn't make a loop or any form of course but where there's a will, there's a way, and I soon found a routine.

About one month after we moved to the mountains, I decided to train for my first marathon. My brother, Chad, and sister, Amy, were both signed up for the Disney marathon and I was excited at the idea of running it with them! I had wanted to run a marathon for a long time before but between having babies and surgery, I never felt that the timing was right. I secured a spot in the race just eight weeks before the big day, which left me with insufficient time to train. I hadn't run over four miles in a long time but somehow convinced myself that I could safely get from running four miles to 26 miles in just two months. I remember feeling so accomplished when I ran for a solid hour on one of my training runs. I ran up and down the same dead-end paths over and over on campus until my watch hit 60 minutes. It was terribly redundant, but I pushed through and soaked in the feeling of accomplishment I felt inside.

For my mom's November birthday, she, my sisters, and I went to New York City for the Macy's Thanksgiving Parade. While we were there, Amy and I put in a 12-miler around Central Park. Passing so many runners, having a partner and actually having space to run was a welcomed break from the training I was squeaking out in Kentucky. While we were in New York City though, we received the news that my beloved Mema had passed away and for the first time in my life, I knew what it felt like to have a broken heart. With the grief came an uptick in periodic heart symptoms I had been experiencing since before my brain surgery. Palpitations and chest pain began to come so regularly that I decided to see a cardiologist when I was back in Kentucky. After several tests, he cleared me for running and I was back at it, using those solo miles to process my loss.

Every week, my long runs jumped in distance with more progression than was wise, so within just a few weeks, I had my first 17-miler on schedule. I was not excited about running all those miles confined to our campus. On the Saturday that my long run was scheduled, we had to make a trip through a state park, crossing a very large mountain for a Christmas ministry party. I had found a way out of doing my long run at the campus! We went to the event, then drove to the base of the mountain where I got out of the car and began to run. Casey and the five kids rode next to me in our Suburban for hours while I traversed the mountain. Our life saver was that kids had all received presents at the party and Casey let them each open a new gift every hour. That gave them something to look forward to as they inched along the icy, mountainous roads. It also gave Casey leverage in case they staged a revolt along the way! It was only 19 degrees that day and the ground was covered in a couple of inches of snow. This Florida girl hates cold weather, had never climbed a mountain, had never run that far, and had little experience even walking in snow or on ice. But somehow, I forged ahead, sometimes having to use my hands to help me climb the steep grades. Occasionally, my steps would lead me to a scenic lookout and my breath would be taken by the impressive view instead of by the cold and hard effort. It was on that run that I learned the value of a climb, finding that without the climb, you never get to the view.

At one point in the run, I noticed that I was running alongside bear tracks. There was a large set and a small set, so we quickly concluded that a mama bear and her cub had travelled along the same road just before we did. As I ran next to the Suburban, Casey and I made a game plan in case we came upon the bears. While I ran, I rehearsed in my head how I would grab the door, sling it open, hop in and put the window up, all before the bear could catch me. Occupying my mind with these plans sure made the miles go by faster!

Thinking back on that run solidifies Casey's commitment to me and my goals. He never questioned my decision to train for a marathon in eight weeks (Although at times I wished he had!). He didn't think my plan of getting my 17-miler in while running over a snow covered and bear infested mountain was too absurd to carry out either. While the run had its distinct challenges for me, he may have had the harder job of keeping the kids entertained in the car for the three and a half hours it took me to log those miles.

I felt accomplished having completed the longest run I had attempted to that date. As Casey pulled up to a stop sign at the end of the run, I slowed to a walk and, with a proud smile on my face, headed for the car, which wasn't too far ahead of me. I allowed myself to relish in knowing that in one run, I had climbed thousands of feet, navigated through snow and had even run alongside bear tracks. I was brought back to the present when, while reaching for the car door handle, I stepped on a patch of ice, falling to the ground with a thud. I had run 17 miles through those rough conditions without a single glitch and it was, in true Kitty fashion, on the final, slow steps to the car that I slipped.

I recuperated from my fall and put in one more long run before the race. After just 8 weeks of training and only two long runs, I naively felt sure I was ready to take on the little 26.2 mile run they call a marathon. I was overwhelmed with emotion at the start of the race. As I stood among thirty or forty thousand other runners, watching the pre-race celebration on the jumbotron and the Disney-tastic fireworks display, I couldn't believe I was actually going to run a marathon after all I had been through with my brain malformation. There were days, so many days, that I struggled to care for myself and my family. The dizziness, the head pressure, the surgery, the dependence on others… it all seemed endless when I was walking through it and there I was, about to run a marathon! It felt miraculous and to one runner among thousands, it was. I *was* just one runner, lost in the crowd and the festivities, but I stood frozen, amazed at the journey I had been on and overwhelmingly thankful for being there at that moment, about to take on the marathon distance with the same body that had struggled so greatly. I whispered a prayer of thanks, wiped away my tears of gratitude and lined up with Chad and Amy to start the race.

Although I was thankful for being healthy enough to run a marathon, I had zero respect for the distance and that became apparent by mile one. The three of us excitedly jogged through the first mile together, packed in tightly with thousands of other runners. At the one-mile mark, I looked at them and said with arrogant resolve, "I'm feeling great so I'm going to go on ahead!" If you've ever run a marathon, you're no doubt laughing out loud at my ignorance. I laugh at it now, too! Of course I felt good… it was only mile one! I waved good-bye to my older siblings and took off, weaving in and out of the crowd as if I had an unlimited supply of energy and stamina. When I got to the halfway point, I was still feeling pretty good and, after looking at my watch, determined that if I could just cover the next 13 miles at the same pace that I covered the first 13, then I would finish in under four hours. This would have been an impressive feat for an undertrained, overconfident first-time marathoner.

What I didn't know at the time was that running the second half of the marathon is a completely different beast than running the first half. Reality met me around mile 15 and so did a knee injury that had been brewing for about four weeks leading up to the race. The knee issue was no doubt from adding too many miles too quickly. I had been aware of it but just pushed through it in training. I had to do the same during the race and it wasn't pretty. The last nine miles of that marathon were grueling as I struggled to just move forward. When I finally saw the finish line come into view, I was sure someone was playing a cruel joke on me, as the finish appeared to be moving farther away with every painful step that I took toward it. I cried like a baby when I finally finished in four hours and thirty minutes- a long way off my self-projected sub-four-hour finish time.

I had never before hurt the way I did after that race. I wanted out of my body but there was no escaping the head-to-toe pain I was feeling. Everything hurt because my limited training had not properly prepared my body for the relentless pounding that the body endures during a marathon. That evening, several family members gathered at my brother's house for a little post-race celebration. While everyone was enjoying the time together in the living room, I laid, quietly moaning, in one of the bedrooms. At one point, my big brother came in and started doing jumping jacks and toe-touches to show me how good he felt after covering the same distance that had left me whimpering like a baby. He and Amy laughed as they told the whole family of my infamous departure at mile one. Siblings are the best at keeping you humble.

I flew back to Kentucky barely able to walk. Casey went between laughter and pity as I hobbled through the airport unable to find comfort in sitting, standing or walking. Just one month after my first marathon, we found out we were expecting another baby, our sixth. My knee hurt through the entire pregnancy, but I couldn't have any treatment because I was pregnant. I used the pregnancy to dial back my running and rehab my knee. I still ran up until my due date but with much moderation.

In October 2007, after having three girls in a row, we welcomed our second boy, Westin Earl. He was our Kentucky boy, born at the midwifery center in eastern Kentucky. In January, with only one 12-miler under my belt between his birth and the race, I ran the Disney marathon, this time with my mom. I trained lightly since I had just had a baby. My training involved running a few miles, going inside to nurse the baby and then going back out to finish the workout. My mom was planning on running 15-minute miles so I felt like this training approach would be enough to cover the distance at that pace. Our goal was a six- or seven-hour finish time, instead of the 4:30 marathon I drug my miserable self through.

Mom and I covered every step of that marathon together and I secretly enjoyed having her all to myself for several hours. Between being one of five kids, having children of my own who wanted her attention, and living 12 hours from her, time like that a rarity. The pace, although steady, was so slow that our support team of family members began to grow concerned as to whether or not we would finish in the seven-hour cutoff time that was strictly enforced by the Disney marathon. I was beginning to wonder, too and couldn't imagine covering all those miles at that pace and not even getting a medal for it. We finally crossed the finish line in six hours and fifty-eight minutes, leaving just two minutes to spare before we would have received a dreaded DNF (Did Not Finish). As it turned out, our supporters' concerns about us not finishing in time were grounded but mom's timing was perfect. I had enjoyed nearly seven hours of alone time with my mom and had snatched my second marathon finish.

When Westin was eight months old, we moved our family to middle Georgia where Casey continued his work with NAMB at a Baptist camp for boys. We bought a house that needed to be relocated to make room for an expanding hospital in a town nearly an hour away. My brother, who had moved there with his family just a short time before we did, gave us three and a half acres to put our "new" house on. He also had a 690 square-foot "cottage" (the term of endearment I gave to the one-bedroom fixer-upper) that we decided the eight of us could live in while we renovated our house. Turns out, we were on the cutting edge of the tiny house movement and we didn't even know it.

On the day the house movers brought our 2,000 square-foot home down our long country road, the kids and I waited by the side of the road to see the spectacle of our future home rolling by on wheels. When we saw the house in its original location, it was a lovely brick home with a brick fireplace and was nearly 3,000 square-feet. The house was too large though to make the 45-mile trip to our house so the house movers had to cut part of it off, which included half of the dining room, the front entryway, a closet and the front door! For safety reasons, they also had to remove all of the brick from the home. The charming brick home that we had seen when we decided to buy it was plastic wrapped and had a gaping hole in it when it came down the road that day.

As the kids and I waited for the house to be brought to our property, we were surprised at how windy and chilly it had gotten. The driveway back to our tiny, temporary house was almost a quarter of a mile long and with the new house bound to show up any moment, none of us wanted to risk the chance of missing it by running all the way back to the "cottage" to get jackets. Gunner, who was nine years old the time, was really into dressing up as an explorer and was in full costume that day, including the apparently essential explorer's backpack. When Gunner had gotten dressed that morning and went to put his empty backpack on his back, he didn't like that his backpack looked empty because that obviously isn't very explorer-like. To fix the problem, he grabbed a good-sized stack of scrap fabric and stuffed it into his pack, making it satisfyingly full.

When Explorer Gunner saw his mom, four sisters, and little brother shivering to stay warm that day, he kindly offered his stash of scrap fabric for us to wrap up in. We each took a piece of the jagged edged scraps and laughed at ourselves as we waited for the house to come over the nearest hill and into view. As part of the preparation for the house to make its way down our road, a sheriff's deputy stopped a couple of oncoming cars that came from the opposite direction. One of the cars decided to make a U-turn and take a detour but the other driver chose to pull over and join us in watching the rare house moving event. We chatted with the friendly man for a few minutes before we saw the house crest the hill in the distance. The house, led by pilot cars, took up both lanes and overlapped both shoulders of the road. With full fanfare from our cheering family, wrapped in rags, the house passed by and made its turn to its final destination. The house looked rough, blue tarps flapped on the roof and hung over the front quarter of the house that had been cut off, while white plastic house wrap hung in wind-tattered shreds all around the house.

When the road was clear, the man who had stopped to watch the move said goodbye and headed back to his car. As he walked away, he stopped at Gunner and put something in his nine-year-old hand, telling him to give it to his mom. That kind man had put over $100 in cash into Gunner's little fist! We were all amazed at the blessing and wondered what prompted that guy to give such a generous gift. I stood in amazement and wonder for a moment before I began slowly scanning the scene around me. We were a family with six children wrapped in rags standing on the side of a country road on a windy day to watch, with extreme excitement, a home roll in that looked like it came from a war-torn area. I wondered no longer but we sure laughed about that story for many years!

Living close to Chad was a dream as he and I picked back up the running routine we had enjoyed together when we both lived in Florida. Hopewell Road, the first road we'd shared since we were dirt covered little kids, soon became our training ground. We challenged each other in distance, pace, and consistency, always finishing a run together in our classic all-out sprint to the finish. It was during this time that I got bitten by the Boston Marathon bug. I had been running for pretty much my whole life and after trashing my legs in one marathon and running a 6:58 in my second, qualifying for Boston seemed like the next logical step, I guess.

I knew the prestige of being a Boston qualifier but had no idea of the pace required to achieve it. When I found that I had to finish 26.2 miles in under three hours and forty minutes, I began to research how to train to get fast enough to do that (That's under 8:30 per mile for 26 miles!). I quickly realized that in order to be fast at long distances, I would need to get faster at short distances and then build up from there. I was getting pretty quick on my feet from running with Chad and began to pound out mile repeats and other workouts on the treadmill while my little ones were napping.

As it usually does, the patience and hard work was paying off and I was getting faster at every distance. I had built up to running a weekly 10-miler to try to add some endurance to my speed work when I found out I was pregnant again. I wasn't the least disappointed about the news and how it would affect my training, and was thrilled to be having another baby. After five babies born in Florida and one in Kentucky, this would be our Georgia Peach. I decided to put my Boston goals on the back burner and returned to my running rules for pregnancy. Since my body was used to those weekly long runs, I kept them up throughout my pregnancy and even ran a half marathon with Chad when I was seven months pregnant. I knew to take it slow and easy, adding in walk breaks when necessary and I proudly crossed the finish line right behind my ever-growing belly. Unfortunately, soon after our race, my brother and his family moved back to Florida to be near Steffanie's family. I lost my running partner, but I did not lose my desire to qualify for the Boston Marathon.

As soon as I recovered from the birth of Emmie Pearl, born in March of 2010, I focused what little energy I had left- after homeschooling, nursing a baby, and raising seven children- on getting into top shape for making a go at running a Boston Qualifying (BQ) marathon. I set my sights on the Space Coast Marathon in Florida in November. Eight months for training for a marathon seemed like a luxury to me after cramming for my other two marathon finishes! I started with an ambitious 10K training plan and during the training, raced a 5K to make sure that my time at that distance would be the right base for building miles upon, while keeping speed. I switched to my marathon plan mid-summer and raced a 10K in early September to test my ability.

The progress I was making was astounding to me. I was crushing the goal times I had determined that I needed to translate into a BQ marathon. I won't paint training for a marathon alone while nursing a baby and raising six other children as anything but challenging. But I was focused on the goal and had the full support of my family so I was soon reminded that where there's a will, there really is a way.

I always woke up before the kids to get my runs in, but as the days grew shorter, I was faced with the issue of not having enough daylight to cover my miles. Casey helped me with this by driving our white 15-passenger van behind me on many of my runs to light my way until the sun came up. One time, while I ran on the long, lonely country road with a van following close behind, a good Samaritan stopped to see if the guy in the van was causing a problem for me. I assured him that it was my husband who was following so closely. I could see how suspicious the situation looked and appreciated the stranger's concern!

Many of my long runs were broken into two segments with me nursing the baby in between. However, when Casey's hunting season and my marathon training collided, I had to get even more creative. Hunting and marathoning training both require early mornings which left us without anyone to watch the kids. Kelsi was old enough and more than responsible enough to be left alone with the kids while I was out on a run, but watching six siblings, one of whom was a new baby, was a tough task that I didn't expect her to do for long periods without someone checking in. So, on some long runs, I would run out a half of a mile from my house, and turn around and go back, logging one mile. This way I was never more than a half of a mile from home and could be waved down to a stop from the kids in our secluded yard if they needed me. On one 17-miler, I ran the entire distance in one-mile segments with frequent check-ins on the kids. I kept a pile of 17 twigs at the end of our driveway and as I completed each mile, I moved a twig out of the pile, which helped me keep track of my distance amidst all of the interruptions.

One of my longest runs was run over the course of an entire morning and some of the afternoon because I had to take care of so many issues with the kids. To keep myself from getting frustrated, I had to remind myself often that raising the children, not running, was my first priority. On another run, Kelsi had each of the kids who could ride a bike meet me at the end of the driveway when I returned from each mile. They would each ride a mile with me and then I would drop them at the end of the driveway, where the next child would join me for another mile. This trading in and out of little bikers helped break up my run and gave me time with each of them.

If my training sounded less than professional, it was. It was borderline insane and was often times comical, but I stuck with it, logging many lone miles out on Hopewell Road. A change started to happen inside of me as I ran. I became tough, running like a machine, mile after mile. By day, I was a mild-mannered housewife- homeschooling, reading bedtime stories and sorting laundry- but in the early morning hours I was a competitor, becoming more unbreakable by the week. Though I wasn't trying for a tough-as-nails approach to running, I was aware that it was happening inside. My focus, my stride and my pace were all driven by an ever-growing desire to become a Boston Qualifier. I already felt like an overcomer for making it back to running after brain surgery, feeling like the sky was the limit for me, but I was completely unaware that there was another problem that had been with me since birth. It was a defect that affected the very organ that was pumping blood to my demanding muscles.

By the time race day arrived, I had shrunk to a 108-pound frame thanks to months of high mileage and exclusively nursing baby Emmie. I was small, but I was fit. Casey drove me to the race where I changed a diaper and nursed Emmie before heading to the start. My brother met us there and brought his bike to travel along the race course to encourage me as I ran. My dad was there too, and the scene began to match the vision of the race that I had pictured in my head while I was running all of those Hopewell Road training miles. Those three men had given me unwavering support and were always behind me in my goals, so it was fitting that they be there at the Space Coast Marathon that day.

In the months leading up to the race, I was clocking times that indicated I could run faster than the requisite 3:40 BQ standard for my age so, based on those times, I decided to aim for a 3:30 finish and took my place at the start with the 3:30 pace group. A pace group is built around a pacer who is a paid runner designated to cross the finish line in the exact time prescribed for the group. Many marathons offer pacers for finish time goals every 5 minutes through the most desired finish times. A pace group is formed when runners, like me, line up with the pacer that will finish in the goal time they're aiming for. Pace groups are valuable because they provide accountability, steady pacing and encouragement along the course.

At the starting line, the runners in my pace group exchanged typical pre-race banter as we waited for the starting gun. The conversation, as it often does among runners, quickly turned to shoes. Everyone in the group agreed that real runners didn't wear a certain brand until I chimed in to point out that I was wearing that brand. This was followed by awkward silence and then the other runners in the group picked the conversation back up, discussing how often they switch out their running shoes. It's general knowledge in the running community that a dedicated runner only puts a few hundred miles on a pair of shoes until they're forced into retirement and a new $150 pair of shoes is bought. I didn't disagree with this practice, but with seven children and living on missionary support, I was afforded just one pair of running shoes per year, which Casey bought me for my birthday every year. By the time our pace group lined up for the November race start, I had been wearing the same pair of shoes since February. The other runners were shocked to hear this (as well as to hear that I had seven children!) and between that and the fact that I was wearing 'non-runner' shoes that were older than my youngest baby, I was unanimously dubbed "most-likely-to-be-the-first-to-drop-out-of-the-pace-group." I silently reminded myself that the race was about preparation and heart, not about the shoes. With that dose of self-encouragement, the starting gun sounded, and my first Boston qualifying attempt had begun.

As we raced along the scenic waterfront racecourse, runners in our pace group began to drop off, one by one. My dad, who had cheered me on in those beauty pageants in my early years was still cheering on his baby girl, this time in a different event. By mile 18, fueled by support from Casey, Chad, and my dad, I was the only runner left running with our pacer. Go figure. It's wasn't about the shoes after all. My last couple of miles were rough and I, too, ended up falling behind our pacer but I finished in 3:32, good enough for a Boston Qualifier and good enough for second place in my age group. I took the stage to receive my award with Emmie strapped to me in a baby carrier. I had just finished nursing her before they called my name. Such is the life of a running mom.

Because my qualifier was in November, which was 2 months after the Boston Marathon registration cutoff, it would be a year and a half before I would actually get to go to Boston to run in the prestigious race. During that time, I nabbed another qualifier, finishing in almost the exact same finishing time. When April 2012 rolled around, Casey and I were ready for a trip away together and I was thrilled to be running the world's most historic race.

In the six months leading up to the marathon, I was plagued with a cold that had settled in my chest, so I didn't get in a good training cycle before heading to Boston. I decided I would just go and enjoy the race course, without worrying about my finish time. This turned out to be a blessing because the weather on race day ended up topping out at 89 degrees, one of the top ten hottest days in the history of the race. Temperatures that high are extremely dangerous for endurance runners so I knew that even if I had been well trained for the run, I would have been severely hindered by such scorching weather. The morning of the race, I met a fellow runner, Bernard, who, because of shin splints, also had less-than-stellar training leading up to race day and was just there for the accomplishment of finishing it. Bernard and I decided to run together and, over the course of 26.2 miles, we became fast friends. We learned about each other's families and the qualifiers that gave us the opportunity to step up to the Boston Marathon starting line. By mile seven, Bernard's stomach starting cramping- a telltale sign of dehydration- and he began vomiting. Despite the hardships he was facing, we stayed together for the entire race, finishing in 4:30. It was slow compared to what it took for each of us to get qualified, but it was a much easier and more enjoyable 4:30 than I had run during my first marathon at Disney just a few years before!

Of course, Casey was at the finish line and cheered me on with so much pride that I thought he might burst. He had arrived at the finish area four hours before the race to secure a good spot. We found each other after the race, and I introduced him to Bernard. We all agreed to stay in touch as we said our goodbyes. I left the finish area knowing that because of my second qualifier, I had a spot in the 2013 race and hoped I would be able to make it back to cross that iconic finish line once more.

5

Courage to Grieve

It was late December 2012 and things were rough at the Robinson house. We had seven kids ranging in age from 2-15 and everyone one of us had a stomach bug that would not relent. Our days were consumed with washing sheets, rotating puke buckets and spraying Lysol. Lots of Lysol. To make matters worse, right before we got sick, we bought three, days-old calves that were on the brink of death by the time they were delivered to our house, which probably explains why we bought them for only ten dollars each! Three times a day, one of us would emerge from our stomach bug induced stupor and brave the winter weather to feed the trio of calves who were, coincidentally, also too weak to eat.

About one week into it the ordeal, the bug hit me, and I started to feel sick. No vomiting though, just nausea. And interestingly, my nausea was mostly in the morning. Even after the stomach bug cleared the house a few weeks later, my nausea persisted. This bug started to feel like the one I'd had seven times before. I decided to take a pregnancy test. The good news was that I didn't have the stomach bug and what should have been even better news was that I was indeed pregnant with our eighth baby.

I am a celebrator of life and have been completely overjoyed with the news of each of my other pregnancies. I felt unworthy of such amazing gifts, so I really struggled when I saw those two little pink lines show up on this pregnancy test and I wasn't elated. Feeling disappointed with the news of a new life growing inside of mine was unfamiliar territory.

This news came at a time when the circumstances surrounding us were bleak. I was weary from taking care of so many "patients" that month and I felt overwhelmed by the responsibility that was on my shoulders to keep everything afloat. Out of everyone in the family, Casey had been the sickest that dreary December, so he was unable to work. Our missionary support had dwindled drastically to the point that it was almost non-existent and to be honest, we were having a hard time putting food on the table for our already large family.

On top of that, I couldn't shake the remembrance of the severe heart symptoms I faced during my last pregnancy. Even though doctors had told me that everything was fine, there were many days during my pregnancy with Emmie, my seventh, that I felt my heart was just going to stop. I recall telling my best friend, Celia, that I thought we would be done at seven children because I didn't think my heart could handle another pregnancy. Of course, I didn't have any official medical diagnosis for such a conclusion so to outsiders who knew I ran a 2:15 half marathon 32 weeks into my pregnancy with Emmie, everything looked perfect. Only I knew what it felt like to have my heart fall into irregular rhythms, and I wasn't sure that I could handle it again.

More often than not, our lack of faith and despair comes from focusing only on our temporary situations and that's what had me struggling to come to terms with the news of my latest pregnancy. All I could see was a bare pantry, a sickly husband who could hardly walk to the car, let alone work, and a house full of growing children who needed their momma alive. These were *very* real concerns, so I don't discount them. But according to Hebrews Chapter 11, the definition of faith is the substance of things hoped for, the evidence of things unseen. I had to trust God for the things I couldn't see in this situation. I had to learn to trust that he would continue to provide for us, just as he always had. I had to trust him with my health. He always had been, and always will be, faithful. I knew he wouldn't stop being faithful during the one situation that I couldn't see the other side of. I also had to believe, with action, that he created this child for a reason and that, despite circumstances surrounding the timing of this news, he had a bigger plan.

Being planned *and* wanted aren't what makes a child a good gift. Every child is a blessing whether it comes into this world under stable or difficult circumstances. I *knew* all of this, but I had to live out that faith. I felt guilty for even having to work on it. I felt guilty for not being excited so I vowed not to share the news with family and friends until I could tell them with excitement in my voice and true joy in my heart.

After a couple of weeks, my heart started to change, and joy began to grow towards this precious baby forming inside of me. Casey and I finally excitedly told our loved ones, which is not always an easy task when it's your eighth baby. Not surprisingly, in a world that often sees children as a burden instead of a blessing, the responses from well-meaning friends and family weren't always encouraging. Knowing this was part of the reason that I knew *I* had to at least be excited as we spread the word.

I continued to run during this pregnancy but had decided I wouldn't be going to Boston in the following spring since at the time of the 2013 Boston Marathon, I would have been halfway through my pregnancy. Besides sticking to my pregnant-while-running rules that my doctor and I had agreed on years earlier, there was one last rule that I made up myself: no marathons. I didn't even entertain the thought of going to Boston that year. My excitement about the pregnancy was growing, and I decided that having a baby was well worth wasting a hard-earned Boston qualification. Pregnancy sickness had waned early on and I was uncharacteristically energetic. In fact, there were many days that I didn't even feel pregnant at all.

After seven uncomplicated, natural hospital births, including one water birth and two births attended by midwives, I was thrilled that Casey had finally agreed to let me have a home birth with our little number eight. I found a local midwife, Carlene, who would help make this dream of mine a reality. When I was ten weeks pregnant, I went to my first prenatal appointment with the midwife, which was in a welcoming and comfortable office at her home. Since I'd been able to hear all of our babies' heartbeats externally by that point in the pregnancy, Casey and I brought along a few of the kids to hear their newest little sibling's heartbeat. After answering Carlene's typical pregnancy questions, I laid back on the examining table. Carlene put the doppler wand on my belly and moved it around, searching for those often hard-to-detect fetal tones. I was smiling in anticipation as Casey was whispering to the kids to get them pumped up for the big moment. Sadly, that big moment never came. My countenance fell as the minutes ticked on and there was still no heartbeat. Casey and the kids grew quiet, in part so we could hear better but also because he didn't know what to say. Carlene was encouraging as she searched, but after several minutes, she put the wand down and examined my belly. "Are you sure about your dates? Because you don't feel like ten weeks along. Maybe you're not as far along as you thought and that's why we can't hear anything." No, I knew my dates and I began to realize why this pregnancy had felt so different from the others.

At that moment, hope and despair were embattled within me. I wanted so badly to hope for the best and believe that the baby was fine, but the reality of my lack of pregnancy symptoms couldn't be dismissed and that grieved me greatly. I struggled to let hope win, but tears were brimming in my eyes, my throat was swelling, and I couldn't get past the despair that was overtaking me.

The next day we drove to a doctor's office for an ultrasound. The drive there was quiet and heavy. Neither Casey nor I knew what to say. Inside, I was still fighting to let hope win because hope was all I had. The outcome was out of my hands, but I couldn't let it slip away without a fight. Casey and I sat in an OB/GYN office surrounded by pregnancy magazines with pictures of glowing mamas with growing bellies. Even though I had the blessing of being that glowing mama seven times, I hated the thought of losing this baby. My stomach was in knots as I wanted so badly to hope I would be a glowing pregnant woman once more. At the same time, I fought back thoughts that told me I would be experiencing death, not life, with this baby. I filled out paperwork, heard my name get called, changed into a paper gown, all while putting on pleasantries on the outside but still fighting for hope on the inside. I laid down on an examining table with Casey by my side in what seemed like a room purposefully darkened and silenced to create the right atmosphere for devastating news. As the sonographer placed the wand on my stomach, I was pleading with God with all that was in me.

In a moment, the silhouette of our tiny, unborn baby was displayed on the screen. We could see the outline of its miraculously formed body but the sign of life- the heartbeat- was gone. The hope I had fought so hard for drained from me as grief took its place. The emotions I felt seeing that lifeless little Robinson on the screen overwhelmed me. I wanted to turn my head away from the screen to avoid the sight but at the same time, I didn't want to turn my eyes away from the only time I would see my little one this side of heaven. I tried to stop the tears until we got to the car but there was nothing I could do to keep the floodgates from opening. I got up and went to the bathroom to gather myself, trying to just get out of the building before I started wailing. Somehow, I forced the words "thank you" from my lips as I rushed past the sonographer. As I made my way down the hall, she called out in a compassionate tone, "Wait, do you want the pictures?" I looked back to see her holding out a short strip of sonogram pictures. I felt like I had been kicked in the gut. *Really? She's asking if I want the pictures of my dead baby?!?! Is she sick?"*

I turned back and looked at her through tear-filled eyes and rudely shook my head before storming out the door. Casey was behind me in the hall and I heard him whispering to her, trying to make up for my abrupt response. I cried the whole way home and then cried for days afterwards. A mound of tissues was growing by my bedside as I tossed tear-smeared wads of sorrow in that direction. One day, Casey came in to try to clean up my pile of snotty Kleenex and I snapped at him, telling him to leave them alone. After he left the room, I searched my heart to try to figure out what that pile of trash meant to me. Why did the thought of cleaning it up bother me so much? The answer came as I cried out to the Lord, "Please Lord, show this pile to my baby and let him know that he was wanted. I wanted him, I really did! Let him know that his passing is filling me with grief, and I would do anything to get him back. All these tears are for him from his mother who loved him already. And Lord, please forgive me for not being happy about this pregnancy from the very beginning. I'm so…

sorry." That was it. The pile of tissues was a physical monument that displayed my extreme guilt for the disappointment I had when I first found out that baby number eight was on the way. And somehow, I felt like if we removed that "monument", there would be nothing to show my baby that he was wanted and that his loss was felt. I knew it didn't make sense. Grief rarely does.

I carried my dead, unborn baby in my womb for 2 more weeks. I refused to have a D and C which is a common procedure done in cases of miscarriage in which the doctor scrapes all of the tissue out of the uterus. I had always leaned towards letting my body do things naturally so that was a big part of my reasoning behind waiting for the miscarriage to happen on its own. I also felt strongly that I was not going to have a procedure done that would end the life of my baby if the sonogram had been wrong. I certainly didn't want to remove the possibility of a miracle happening. And this may sound crazy, but I felt like I needed to *feel* the loss of my baby. I couldn't bear the thought of a medical professional telling me my baby was dead, then putting me to sleep, cleaning me out and waking me up to tell me it was all over. I couldn't understand how that could feel real and how I would be able to process the grief after such a sterile experience in the loss. My other seven children came forth in great pain that I felt every wave of. I never thought bringing a human into the world should be easy. I felt like I needed to feel whatever was to come in passing this one, too. I won't justify that feeling or say that it was right over someone else's approach to dealing with this type of loss. I can only say that it's what felt right for me in that situation and that it was the approach that I believed would bring me the most closure.

So, I waited. Still pregnant but not. Conversations were difficult and awkward with me lacking the language to explain this state in which I was teetering. Part of me wanted my body to go ahead and get it over with and part of me wanted to keep my lifeless child inside of me because once gone we would never be physically close again. And all of me was secretly praying for a miracle. If my processing of the loss seems strange, I make no excuses for the way my finite human mind tried to make sense of my devastation. I only know that the Lord comforted me and sustained me through those weeks and removed the guilt I felt for my initial feelings towards the pregnancy.

I found comfort in the Lord in those dark days. I also found comfort in my other children, but enjoying them became bittersweet. The more I snuggled with them and enjoyed them, the more aware I was of what I was losing in the miscarried child. The Lord also used running to help me work through the grief. In those weeks of waiting to miscarry, I kept up with my daily running routine and in those grief-filled days, that's all it was: routine. Like a robot, I got up, got dressed, laced up my shoes, headed out the door and put one foot in front of the other. That by itself was helpful in a small way. I felt oddly conflicted at times though because for seven pregnancies, I followed my running-while-pregnant-rules for the protection of my unborn baby. I was pregnant so I should have been adhering to those rules. But this baby was dead. Anything I could do to try to protect it and nurture it was all in vain. I could run myself into the ground, collapse in complete dehydrated exhaustion and it wouldn't have made a difference. Thoughts like these often snapped me from my robotic-like state to an awareness of tears streaming down my cheeks. There were several times in those weeks that I found myself bent over on the side of the road, hands on knees, crying uncontrollably. This was healing: doing something so familiar that my mind didn't have to engage. This left my mind free to explore thoughts that needed processing, grief that needed digging up, and comfort that needed to be administered.

It was on one of those runs where my mind was sorting through my heartache that I began to think about the sonogram pictures that I had rejected. At the time, I was deeply offended by the nurse's offer but later, in rhythmic breathing and feet pounding the pavement, I found myself contemplating what those pictures meant to me. They were the only tangible evidence of the brief existence of our baby, and I had rejected them. I had never been through that kind of loss before so I had no way of knowing that what offended me just weeks before would have become a cherished treasure if only I would have kept them.

It was also on those runs that I speculated the types of responses we would get from people when they heard of our loss. From having so many children, we got used to getting a lot of rude comments from inconsiderate people. I naturally expected those same types of responses when we also told people about our loss. I fully anticipated hearing things like, "Well, at least you have seven other children." Or "God knew what you could handle" and "you can always have another one." Yes, we did have seven other children and I was extremely thankful for the gift of motherhood and for each of our blessings. But we have loved each of them as much as someone loves their only child and I had already loved that new baby just as much. Knowing how deeply I was grieving, I had no idea how I would respond if someone brushed off our loss as insignificant just because we had so many children already. While I ran with my legs, my mind ran through the spectrum of responses I could give to those seemingly inevitable hurtful comments.

To my surprise, we never received a single negative comment during our season of loss. Instead, we were showered with love, prayers, condolences and simple acts of kindness that meant the world to us during such a difficult time. Some of our church family in the little town of Musella, Georgia went out of their way to care for us. They brought flowers, meals, a rose plant and even came and sat with me when I needed someone there. Others sent cards and text messages. Steffanie (my sister-in-law) and two long time friends, Amy and Jonatha, sent me a soft blanket from Florida to remind me that they were covering me in prayer. It was hard to be away from them so every time I cuddled up under that soft blanket, I was comforted by thoughts of their enduring friendship.

After three weeks of being in a strange limbo between pregnancy and miscarriage, I began to bleed. I was 13 weeks along, but my baby had been dead for 5 of those weeks. From that point on, I didn't want to be away from Casey. I needed him there when the spotting turned into a miscarriage. As if three weeks of being pregnant- but not- wasn't hard enough, they were followed by seven days of miscarrying- but not. Seven days after the onset of the bleeding, my body finally began to kick into action. What surprised me was that in order to rid my body of the pregnancy, my body went into full-fledge labor. I endured four hours of contractions every two minutes on my bed while Casey went back and forth between tending to my needs and checking on the kids, who were all home.

As I would brace myself and breathe through each contraction, I looked down at my flat stomach and it all felt so fake. I remembered a video Casey and I had seen a couple months before that showed two men hooked up to a machine that would simulate what labor feels like. The video was hilarious as these obviously not-pregnant men went through the throws of labor. Seeing myself laboring but not looking pregnant made me feel just like those two guys. But this time it wasn't funny. I'd been through labor 7 other times and always looked down to see a huge belly tightening with each birth pain. In those labors, I had the promise of a healthy newborn to hold when it was all over and that was enough to give me the strength I needed to endure the pain. Sure, I leaned heavily on the Lord in those times, too and felt him so close to me, but I had some pretty strong motivation through the hours of labor. The miscarriage though was so different and cruel. There was no promise of anything except getting it over with. I wouldn't hold a baby. Casey and I wouldn't stare into a face that was a miraculous combination of our love and DNA. Loved ones weren't excitedly waiting the news. It was just hours of meaningless, painful contractions and bleeding.

Our house was 40 minutes from the nearest medical facility and as my "labor" wore on, the bleeding grew worse. Casey and I had never seen so much blood! We were on the phone several times with the midwife who was telling us what to expect. She reassured us that what I was experiencing was not abnormal and that we didn't need to go to the hospital. After 4 hours, things quieted down so we assumed the horrible ordeal was finally over. Casey and I rested well all night and I spent the next day in bed, recuperating, while Casey took charge of all the kids.

To our shock, the contractions and bleeding started again the next night. I had already lost so much blood the night before, we didn't see how my body could handle going through that again. I could hardly sit up straight and at one point even passed out on the toilet. Once again, we were on the phone with the midwife, wondering if we should be at the hospital. She calmly talked to us through all of the hemorrhaging and told us what to watch for. Casey was in a constant frenzy of changing bed pads, checking on kids, calling the midwife, and keeping me conscious. Finally, with one huge contraction, I knew it was done. I had passed everything Carlene had told me to look for, and then some, and my uterus finally stopped contracting. With relief and complete exhaustion, Casey and I went to bed feeling numb from the extreme suffering. There were no words of comfort. Just mutual silence.

I hoped the next day would be the beginning of my healing, both physically and emotionally, but the next day only brought the realization that I was too weak to even sit up. Though I had already lost so much blood, I was still bleeding. All of my energy had been drained by the back-to-back nights of hemorrhaging. When I still didn't improve, we decided, along with the midwife, that it was time to see a doctor. At that point, I knew I had endured the pain for my child and that there was now physical evidence that this pregnancy was over. If I needed a D and C, I no longer felt any hesitation by the idea of the procedure.

I was referred to a male doctor whom I'd never met. I was so weak that Casey had to help me to the examining room. Once in the room, I lay on the examining room table because sitting up was too exhausting. The doctor came in, sat down, looked at my chart, wheeled himself over to me, and asked blandly, "So, we're having a miscarriage?" If I had had the strength to get up and leave that room that day, I sure would have. How could an experienced OB/GYN who had dealt with such loss countless times, approach a pale and grieving mother with such a flippant remark?

The doctor did a sonogram and found that despite all the bleeding I had endured, there was still more tissue to pass. Because I was already so weak from the blood loss and because the baby had already been dead inside of me for 5 weeks, he felt that we would risk serious infection if we waited this out any longer. I wearily agreed that it was time to get this over with and begin healing, so the next day I went into the hospital for the procedure. I have to admit that the doctor who had hurt my heart with his careless remark the day before was much more compassionate that next day. He came into the pre-op area just to pray with Casey and I before I was put to sleep. Likewise, all of the nurses and hospital staff went out of their way to be caring and empathetic. With one out of every five pregnancies ending in miscarriage, I suspect that not only had they cared for many patients experiencing miscarriage, some of the nurses had most likely experienced it themselves.

I spent the next 6 months living life as fully as I could but openly allowing myself to grieve and heal on the inside. I was always painfully aware of how far along I would have been at any given time and when my due date approached, the grief flared up again. Casey gave me the space I needed on the due date and we spent some time with the kids to have a short, but meaningful, ceremony for the baby.

Sorting through all of the grief and emotions that accompanied this loss was not easy, but it was necessary. It was painful to embrace the feelings, I knew it would have been more detrimental in the long run to stuff them inside. The season was tough but the Lord gave me the strength to endure it, embrace it and heal from it. If I had been given the full script of this ordeal before walking into it, there's no way I would have thought that I had the courage to make it through that deep, dark valley. The courage was there for me though, in small doses, just enough for the day at hand because sometimes that's how courage comes.

6

Courage to Go

It took an entire month for my body to fully recover from the blood loss and trauma of the miscarriage. It was March now and spring was emerging. I began to walk and then run again, allowing the colorful blooms everywhere to encourage my soul to rebloom as well. I was just running a few miles at a time, giving my body the chance to ease back into the familiar routine.

It was that March that my brother and his wife, Steffanie, drove up to our area to run a half marathon that we had run together a few years before. I knew I wasn't ready to cover that distance yet, so Casey and I decided to stay in the same hotel as Chad and Steffanie, just to enjoy some time together and cheer my brother on in the race.

The night before the race, while at the expo, the race bug bit me and I decided to sign up to run with Chad the next morning. I reasoned that I could just run slow and cover the miles. My body knew the distance and I was sure that muscle memory would kick in. The next day, like I'd done so many times before, I lined up at the starting line next to my big brother. There was so much comfort in that moment- in our positions. Shoulder to shoulder, race numbers pinned on and hands on our watches, ready to start them when the gun went off... it all felt so right. I flashed back to our toes lined up to a line we had drawn in our dirt road, mailboxes to the right and a neighbor to our left ready to shout out "Go!" We would take off, giving it everything we had until we reached the next mailbox. I would eat Chad's dust, quite literally, but I would always want to try again. This time, over two decades later, we weren't competing, but we were still little sister and big brother, lined up ready to do it- together.

We ran together for the first ten miles and everything felt right in the world. Chad cracked jokes the entire time which were like balm to my wounded soul. We maintained a steady ten minute-per-mile pace as the miles ticked by. Deciding to run that half marathon the night before, without any proper training may have seemed like an insane idea at the time, but out there running with Chad, it felt like just what I needed. Heading into our eleventh mile, Chad decided to pick up the pace a bit, while I focused on just maintaining our current pace.

With three miles left to go on my own, I had some time on my hands to let the running do what I believe God designed it to do. It allowed me the head space to work through the left over hurt I had yet to sweep away following the miscarriage. With each step, I was processing and with each breath I was remembering. As my body moved through the streets of Albany, GA, the Lord was helping my mind move through the experience: disappointment, excitement, loss, guilt, hurt, pain and healing. Finally, the healing was coming full circle. I could feel it welling up inside of me just as surely as I could feel the cold March air filling my lungs and as fully as I could feel the lactic acid burning in my muscles. But while the air and the acid stung, the healing soothed. As I headed towards the finishing shoot of the race, I was snapped back into the moment and made those final strides with tears streaming down my red cheeks. I crossed the line and one final wave of emotion flooded from me. I cried, took a few steps and then cried some more. These tears were tears of healing, comfort and relief. I had finished the race, yes, but I had also allowed myself the all-encompassing experience of the grief and healing that was an entirely different kind of finish line. Crossing that finish line took a different kind of courage than I had ever known but, yielded to him, the Lord gave me just what I needed, as I needed it.

My brother was waiting for me when I finally crossed the finish line. When he found me, I was doubled over, hands on my knees, in tears and he seemed to understand. No asking, "What's wrong?" Just a comforting hand on the back and complete understanding. That's how it has always been between us.

When I got back from the race in Albany, there was an interesting piece of mail waiting for me. It was my registration packet for the 2013 Boston Marathon, which was just 2 weeks away. There's something powerful about getting a packet from the Boston Athletic Association with your name on it. There's something even more amazing about opening the package and pulling out your race number. Even though I had worked for several grueling months to qualify for that race, running it hadn't crossed my mind since I found out I was pregnant. I had resolved to focus on a healthy pregnancy and put my dreams of once more running the streets of Boston to rest. I had paid the $150 registration fee back in September so I should have been expecting that packet. However, I was actually surprised when it arrived. I tore open the over-sized envelope and reaching in, pulled out my race bib. I stood with that race number in my trembling hands and just kept thinking *I have a race number. I have a race number.* It's as though they were expecting me to show up. All I had to do was get to Boston, pin the bib on and I could run the prestigious Boston Marathon. I had worked so hard for it but there I stood, shocked that it was in my hands. I had spent the past few months being pregnant, losing a baby and just trying to regain strength so standing there with my race number in my hands, the competitor who earned that race number seemed so far away. Yet that girl who stood in her dining room, looking down at her number was stronger than the girl who had earned it.

My mind began to whirl with potential plans and thoughts on how to get to the 2013 Boston Marathon wearing my race number. I showed my race packet to Casey and he immediately began picturing me at that race. He started asking me questions, wondering if I even wanted to go and within a few minutes, we were brainstorming about how to get me there. I can't remember a time in the past 24 years of being with Casey that he didn't support me 100% so I wasn't surprised when he wholeheartedly encouraged me to go. I hadn't trained a bit, nor did I have an airline ticket or a hotel room… or even transportation in Boston. But he was completely behind me in this crazy idea- a crazy idea that had quickly become a plan. His only stipulation? I must promise to buy a cell phone to take with me on the trip. I was one of the final holdouts on cellphones and refused to carry one with me. But I agreed and, despite the phone issue, was, as always, thankful for his support.

Casey had never held back when it came to dreaming big for me but we knew that he and I couldn't go together. In the middle of the miscarriage crisis, we had moved to serve at a Christian camp that was for underprivileged inner-city kids. Casey was in the throes of adapting to his new workload there and couldn't get away. We also knew that we couldn't afford two plane tickets to Massachusetts at such late notice and didn't have anyone to watch our children. I decided to call my mom and my sister,

Amy and ask them to go with me. Despite the fact that the marathon was only two weeks away, they both said they were in. Within 24 hours, all three of us had plane tickets and a hotel room to share. A crazy idea that rapidly turned into a plan had become a reality! As sad as I was that Casey wouldn't be at the finish line waiting for me again that year, my mom, sister and I were excited about the adventure we were about to together.

I knew with only 2 weeks to go before the race, there wouldn't be any training going on for me. I would run some easy miles over those 14 days and then just go cover the distance on the streets of Boston. Like most marathons, the Boston Marathon keeps the course open for 7 hours and I knew I could go 26.2 miles in that time, even without actually training. I made up my mind to not even look at a watch. I would just enjoy. Enjoy the spirit of Boston on Patriot's Day. Enjoy the cheering crowds. Enjoy the opportunity and enjoy the fruit of the hard work it took to qualify for the marathon in the first place. With no training, except for one slow and therapeutic half-marathon, I was going back to Boston.

7

Boston Courage

Two weeks later, on Sunday morning, April 14, 2013, the day before the marathon, I was jumping out of bed early, excited to head to the airport. Casey and I didn't have anyone living nearby who could watch the kids so we loaded all seven of our sleepy children into our white 15-passenger van under a starry, pre-dawn sky. Most of the kids fell back asleep as we made our way toward the Atlanta airport. When we were about 30 minutes from the airport, our van started acting up so badly that it forced an emergency stop at a gas station off the interstate. Casey surveyed the engine and determined that the van was no longer drivable. I couldn't believe it! My mom and sister were already on separate flights from Florida to Boston to watch me run in Bean Town and I didn't even know how I was going to get there. They were only going because I talked them into a last-minute trip and now it looked as if I may not even be there. If I did miraculously make it to the airport, we still had no idea how Casey and all the kids would get home. True to Casey's character, his first priority was to get me on my flight. We called several taxi services but soon learned that most drivers weren't too excited about getting up in the dark hours of a Sunday morning to get someone to the airport on last minute's notice.

We finally found a driver who could take me. Casey then contacted a friend who was going to help get Casey, the 15-passenger van and seven children back home. At that point, our main concern was whether or not I could even get to the airport on time. We had been at the gas station for at least 30 minutes before we secured a ride and it took the driver another 25 minutes to get to me. I have to admit, I felt a little unsure about getting in the backseat of a car with a driver whose number I got from a stranger standing behind the counter of a shady looking gas station. That guy was my only chance to make it in time though, so with lots of silent prayers, he picked me up and I was whisked away in the back seat of an unmarked "taxi." As we left the gas station parking lot, I peered through the window and felt like the mother-of-the-year reject, leaving my family more than an hour from home with a broken-down van in a dark gas station parking lot while I went off to chasing dreams.

If all of that had to happen so I could spend 40 minutes in the car with my driver, then it was worth it. That man turned out to be a follower of Christ who had his life turned upside down during the recession of 2008. Through the personal financial loss that he experienced, he found a saving relationship with Jesus! Even though he went from a New York City real estate investor to a middle Georgia taxi driver, he said was happier than he had ever been in his life because his joy came from the Lord, not from his wealth or worldly success. With him sharing what the Lord had done in his life, the cab drive that could have been filled with worry and anxiety was peaceful and encouraging. I sincerely thanked him, snatched my suitcase out of the car and sprinted to my departing gate at the busiest airport in the world.

When I arrived at my gate, the doors had already closed. The plane was set to depart in less than three minutes. My whole morning had come down to three minutes! Just a few changes to the story and I could have been three minutes too late and would have missed my flight to Boston. I thanked the Lord for allowing me to get there on time right after I thanked the attendants for still letting me board the plane!

From the moment I got off the plane in Boston, I remembered how much the city turns on the big welcome for the athletes who converge on the area for the weekend. Beginning with the airport, there are banners, flags and posters up all over the city that celebrate the spirit of the marathon and the runners who come from all over the world to race it. Somehow the city of Boston makes each of the 30,000 marathon runners feel special which was a big reason I was aching to go back that year. My mom and sister came in on their respective flights and we were immediately caught up in the excitement of the city and the big race. We took pictures in front of posters, talked to other runners, feeling every bit of the magic that the Boston Marathon presents.

We got to Boston just in time to go straight to the famed Boston Marathon Expo where over 200 vendors set up booths to support the running community. With nearly 100,000 people making their way to the expo every year, it's a huge event. It was at this expo that runners were able to pick up their official, long-sleeve Adidas race shirt to commemorate participation in the world's oldest marathon. The Boston Athletic Association (BAA) also put all 30,000 runners' names on one poster and gave copies of it out to all of the participants. Oval "26.2" stickers with the BAA logo on them were coveted freebies as well. There were running clinics, free samples and bleachers set up for watching videos on past stories from the historic race. Boston-specific merchandise also enticed athletes at every turn. For a runner, the

Boston Marathon Expo is a candy store, Christmas, and birthday party all rolled into one, running-themed package.

Displayed on the walls of the expo are framed samples of all of the Boston Marathon jackets from over the years. While the race dates back to 1897, the jackets have only been available for runners since 1991. And of course, there's a booth where runners can buy the current year's jacket, as well. I've heard it said that if running is a cult then the Boston Marathon is its temple and the Boston Marathon jacket is its priestly garment. When Casey and I went to Boston in 2012, I drooled over that year's edition of the race jacket. Unfortunately, with a price tag of over $100, we couldn't afford the luxury of buying one. This year, when Casey knew I was going back in two weeks, he began to secretly search online for a 2012 jacket for me. Surprisingly, he found one in my size at a reasonable price and it arrived just in time for me to get it before I left on my trip with Mom and Amy. It meant so much to me to be able to wear my jacket in Boston and, in a way, it was a reminder for me that even though Casey wasn't physically there with me that year, he was always thinking of me and would always be my biggest fan.

The only hotel we could find at such last-minute notice was a bit out of town but right on the water. It was cozy and inviting, even if the location was a tad inconvenient. After getting settled into our room, we went to the hotel restaurant to down some requisite pre-race pasta and to discuss race-day plans.

Between plates of pesto covered pasta, my mom and Amy had the race map and the "T" (Boston's subway system) schedule spread out on the table so they could strategize. I suggested that they just get up early and just head to the finish line. That's what Casey did the year before and he had a great spot right at the finish line to see me come through it. Because he got there so early, he was able to see all the elite runners come through as a bonus. Mom and Amy went on with their plans to cheer me on at mile 17 and then again at mile 21 before heading to watch me cross the finish line on Boylston Street. Once again, I interjected. They had no idea how busy the streets of Boston would be the next morning and I thought it would be near impossible for them to navigate around the city and still make it to the finish line by the time I arrived. They continued planning as I insisted that they didn't need to go through all of that trouble to see me on the course. They just needed to be at the finish line. My sister finally looked at me and said, "Kitty, I didn't come all the way to Boston just to see you finish. I want to be there to cheer you on along the way." My mom agreed. With both of them having completed marathons themselves, they knew how encouraging it was for a runner to see some familiar cheering fans along the 26.2-mile route. I sighed and gave in, but in my mind, I still felt like they were making the wrong decision.

After wondering if I'd ever run again after brain surgery all those years ago, I still felt like I was in a dream seeing how far I'd come. I couldn't believe I was in line yet again to take a school bus to the Athlete's Village the next morning. The Boston Marathon is a point-to-point course, which means it starts in one place and then finishes at another site, 26.2 miles away. This is a unique set up as many races start and finish in the same location which makes the logistics of the race much more manageable. In order to pull off the point-to-point run, the BAA starts bussing runners to the starting line in the wee hours of the morning causing the race to start much later than most marathons. I boarded the bus to the long ride out to Hopkinton Common, where the race begins. Riding the 26 miles in a bus made me aware of just how long the distance was. I shuddered knowing that I would have to run that distance back to Boston and all on very little training. Once at the Athlete's Village, a staging area in Hopkinton, I waited with thousands of other runners for my call to the starting line. The Athlete's Village had refreshments, plenty of porta-potties, and a tent with physical therapy students offering free massages. Most importantly it offered a place for runners to connect and share how they made it to Hopkinton.

I'd been at the Athletes Village the year before but the spectacle of it all felt fresh and new. I was excited to be there but inside I really didn't feel like I belonged. I hadn't trained seriously for months which left me feeling like I wasn't a Boston-quality runner. Though I'm normally pretty outgoing and love meeting new people like I had at the previous year's marathon, that year I felt out of place, so I kept to myself. After getting my first-ever massage, I found a shady spot in the grass to doze off. (Being able to fall asleep just about anytime and anywhere is a gift I have.) All around me were tens of thousands of the world's best amateur runners stretching, warming up, talking to each other, and getting into their mental "zones". The weather was perfect for a great marathon. Excitement was in the air.

All of this was going on around me and there I lay, drifting in and out of sleep, waiting to hear the announcer call my starting wave. With so many runners, the Boston Marathon has runners start in groups called corrals. The corrals are given different start times within four different waves, which creates a staggered wave of runners making their way out of Hopkinton Common and towards Boston. Corrals are determined by runners' qualifying race times so that racers start with other similarly paced athletes. It turned out that my wave was called while I was sleeping. In fact, when I woke up and looked around, the entire Athlete's Village was empty of competitors, meaning that all the other waves had already been called, too. Every single runner was gone. I surveyed the area: an abundance of trash flapped on the grass, propelled by the breeze. Well-used porta-potty doors swung back and forth making rhythmic slamming sounds. Trash cans over-flowed but not a single other runner was in sight. Out of tens of thousands of runners, I was the very last one there and had missed my start time. Typical. Just like the elementary school Kitty who sprinted towards the bus stop, dropping and chasing a watermelon along the way, I was late again, this time running towards the bus where I had to hand over my gear bag before I could go to the starting line.

The BAA had buses that were designated to carry all of the athletes' gear bags for pickup at the finish area. The buses were just pulling out but I made it to the one with my assigned number and tossed my gear bag up into a volunteer's hands that were reaching out the window to catch it. As she made the catch, the bus was already rolling out of the parking lot. I ran to make it to my plane on time, and now I ran to make it to my starting wave, all so I could run to the finish line of the Boston Marathon. Some people will always be running late.

My late race start mimicked the bad dreams I'd had many times on the night before any big race. I would dream of not being prepared, arriving late, or missing the race altogether. Having my racing nightmares come true would have been terrible on any other day. but on that Monday, April 15, 2013, I wasn't really racing. Yes, I intended to cover the full 26.2 miles, but I planned to do it at a nice, easy pace, taking walk breaks, enjoying every step of the historic course.

Aside from my late start, that Monday in Boston was a superb racing day. Unlike the record-breaking heat we experienced the year before, the weather was marathon perfect. As I made my way to the start, I joined the throngs of runners who, though hopefully more prepared, were just as excited as I was. I made my way to the right side of the road and, upon seeing some military personnel staffing the race, quickly decided on a new goal for the race. In addition to keeping it slow, taking walk breaks and enjoying myself, I decided to stop and thank every officer- police or military- I saw working the race route. I did it out of a desire to express gratitude for their presence and found that doing so also added to the reward of the experience for me.

With my laid-back approach to the race, my late start and my mission to thank all the servicemen and women I would find, I was way behind the three and a half hour finishing time that got me to the Boston Marathon in the first place. Had I started on time and didn't stop to express my gratitude, I could have realistically expected to finish the marathon in around 4 and a half hours, considering that I hadn't trained at all. Remembering that it was the miscarriage that had me ill-prepared for a marathon in the first place, I accepted the slower times and didn't mind slowing it down even more with my new race day game plan.

Running the Boston marathon "just for fun" may sound crazy to anyone daunted by the idea of covering 26.2 miles on foot. But for me, it was incredibly freeing and enjoyable to run without even looking at my watch. On Patriot's Day every year in Boston, more than a half of a million wildly cheering fans line the race route to propel the runners on to victory. With that many spectators, the Boston Marathon is the most widely viewed sports event in New England. Although I was just one insignificant runner out of 30,000 others, the fans had me feeling like they were only there to cheer me on. Their encouragement and support was unmatched and infectious. The entire race course was lined with fans, with some more popular areas boasting spectators three or four people deep. Fans were holding signs, cheering with all their might and even handing out food and drinks. Until I came to my mom and sister at mile 17, not one person on that race route knew me, yet I felt like I was one of Boston's most popular runners. That's the magic of the Boston Marathon.

Right before mile 21, where I anticipated seeing my support team again, I remember thinking what a perfect Marathon Monday it had been. The weather was glorious, the crowds were amazing, the pace was comfortable. I was truly enjoying every step of my journey so far. Things only got better when I saw my mom and sister proudly cheering for me at mile 21. Their faces reflected the same elated emotion I felt. I was wearing a race belt which is basically an athletic twist on a fanny pack. It had a pocket in it, which held my phone. This was the first time in my life I had ever run with a phone and only had it with me because I had promised Casey that I would carry it with me. I had stashed a couple of energy gel packs in my race belt, too, which I had used up by the 21-mile mark. I was feeling so strong at that point in the race that I was ready to just cruise to the finish line. Since I felt like I had fulfilled Casey's request by carrying the phone for almost the entire race, I was ready to be freed of the fanny pack for the last bit of the run. I unhooked the belt from around my waist and handed it off to my sister to hold for me. We exchanged high-fives and huge cheesy grins and then I was off to cover the final five miles, unhindered.

Soon after that now infamous handoff, I saw an official photographer on the race course. It's my habit of making sure my race number is visible whenever I see a photographer on a race course, but this time when I looked down to check, I was shocked to see that my race number was gone! Instead of pinning my race number to my clothing like I normally did, I had attached it to my race belt, which had two little spots to attach the top corners of my racing bib. When I handed off my belt to Amy, I had also absent-mindedly given her my race number! My official bib was the only way for me to be identified on the course as a registered runner. Without it, I could be pulled off the course, accused of being a "bandit runner." Bandit runners are unofficial runners who just jump onto a race course, take advantage of the course set-up and support, all without paying a cent for the services. The practice is a disgrace to the running community and there I was, running like a bandit with no race number. Worse than that, my electronic timing chip was embedded in my race bib so without it, I would receive a DNF (Did Not Finish) instead of an official finishing time. After covering 26.2 miles, there would be no record of me actually covering the distance. "Typical Kitty" struck again, giving her bib away in the middle of a race and of all races, the Boston Marathon!

The moment I realized that I had given my race number away, I turned around and sprinted back toward the intersection where I last saw my mom and Amy. Their plan from where we made the handoff was to get to the finish line before I did. As I ran against every other runner in the race, I had no guarantee that the girls would still be where I last saw them. Thankfully, my sister had noticed that she had my race number and had already begun a sprint toward me. What should have been a quick trip for them from mile 21 to the finish had been delayed by my mistake.

Amy and I finally caught up to each other. She handed me the pack and I wrapped the race belt around my waist, clipping it back on. I was, once again, an official runner in the 2013 Boston Marathon, joining the masses running towards the finish line. As my dad had taught me, I laughed inside at my mindlessness and at yet another unusual situation it had put me in. I breathed in the crisp Boston air, stopped to thank volunteers, and wondered if other runners were having as great of a time as I was. The crowds were invigorating. I was thankful for being there as I began to debate my strategy for the last few miles. I felt so good that I knew I could pick up the pace a little and finish strong, but I was enjoying myself so much that I didn't want to rush the moment. For the first time in my life, I didn't want the race to end.

I was jerked from my internal debate by the ringing of the phone that Casey had insisted I bring with me. I pulled it out of my zipper pouch to answer it, feeling very strange to be talking on the phone while running in the Boston Marathon.

"Hello?" I more asked than greeted.

"Hey, are you OK?" Casey asked in a worried tone.

"Yeah, I'm doing awesome! Just a few miles left and I feel great, Why?"

"Someone just called me and said they heard on the news that something bad happened at the finish line there. You need to be careful," he warned.

I looked around at the very fluid scene around me. Spectators were packed in several layers deep and they were cheering on the runners with immeasurable enthusiasm. The race route was dotted with other runners, all making their way towards the finish line. Everything seemed as normal as Marathon Monday in Boston could be. "I don't know what you're talking about, but everything is fine here," I replied with confidence.

"OK, just be careful!" he instructed.

Brushing the warning quickly away, I kept moving forward, refocusing my attention on the energy around me. Casey was in North Carolina with his parents and the friend who called him with the news was in Georgia, where we lived. I didn't understand how someone from another state was trying to tell me what was happening. I was in Boston, on the race route and everything was fine. Completely fine. Better than fine- it was exhilarating. I was running the Boston Marathon! I felt the phone buzz in the race belt pocket. *This was getting annoying*, I thought. *Why did I ever agree to run with a phone?* I pulled it out and read a text from Casey: "Whatever happened at the finish line is serious." I was confused. How was someone so far away telling me what was happening right around me? Then, another text came in:

"There's been an explosion at the finish line. PLEASE BE CAREFUL!"

Feeling confused, I scanned the spectators and found a police officer. I had been making this scan the entire race, looking for emergency personnel to thank. This time, instead of thanking the officer, I was questioning him. "Is it true?" I asked, breathlessly. "Is it true? Was there an explosion at the finish line?" I looked in his eyes and read the answer even before the single word escaped his lips.

"Yes."

"What do I do?" I asked as if I was the only one in the race.

"Just keep running," he said. "They're rerouting the finish line." I thanked him, making it the last opportunity I would have that day to thank anymore of the officers who would be put through a living hell in the hours and days to come.

Doing as instructed, I just kept running. As I pressed on, assuming the explosion was related to a gas leak or some other innocent accident, I silently prayed for the safety of those who were in danger. Within minutes, I noticed a change in the crowds. The cheering had died down, people were on their phones and a sense of awareness came over the masses. They knew. The spectators knew. Confusion began to replace the enthusiasm. The runners, however, had no idea. Unlike my unusual decision to run with a phone, most of the other runners didn't have phones and were disconnected from any news updates. They, too, just kept on running. There were still thousands of us out there on the course, unknowingly running towards the chaos that was playing out at the finish line.

Just under a mile from the finish, I prepared to make the final two turns of the race course: right on Hereford, left on

Boylston. These two turns have become a bit of a catchphrase in the running community, even spawning a running apparel line by the same name, celebrating those famous last turns into downtown Boston and to the finish line. At the expo I had held a kelly green t-shirt with a "Right on Hereford, Left on Boylston" print on it. I considered buying it but the cheaper side of me won out and I returned it to the rack, having no idea that out of the 26.2-mile Boston Marathon course, those would be the only two turns I wouldn't make in the race that year. I would not take a right on Hereford Street nor take a left onto Boylston Avenue. Instead, I would reach a wall of exhausted runners who, like me, had run over 25 miles, just to reach a terrorizing scene and be turned back. Back to where? We had no idea. Like one solid wave that continually consumed more runners as they approached it, the tide of the race had turned, leaving no clear indication of when the wave would dissipate.

In a moment, I went from being a runner just about to finish the most prestigious marathon in the world to being one of thousands of confused and weary runners not knowing what to do next. Marathon finishers are normally given mylar "space blankets" to wrap around their shoulders to prevent hypothermia. Once crossing the finish line, they also have access to fluids, refreshments and medical support, if needed. At that point in the horror, our minor medical needs couldn't compare with the overwhelming rush of victims that filled the medical tents, normally reserved for runners, so we were understandably left to fend for ourselves.

It wasn't unusual for me to be extremely weak and on the verge of passing out once finishing 26.2 miles. When I ran Boston the year before, I had to fight to stay conscious for some time after the race. That year, in 2012, on the hot and muggy subway ride back to the hotel, I was still struggling when a random stranger frantically dug through her purse to find me a mint to sniff and suck on to try to help me keep upright. She had seen the color drain from my face and came to my aid. This time, in 2013, the year of the bombing, I had run nearly the full marathon distance and, instead of being met with typical post-marathon race support, I found myself on the unfamiliar streets of Boston, unsupported, surrounded by crowds of other runners in the same condition. Yet this time, I had a strength and clarity that was completely uncharacteristic of me after putting so much stress on my body. More than that, in the midst of extreme chaos, I was flooded with peace; peace that was so abundant that it flowed over to others. The Lord used me to comfort others in small ways that I hope provided peace to them in such a terrible time. I truly believe the Lord met me- a lone, fatigued runner- and gave me a strength and courage that, to this day, I cannot explain, apart from giving the Lord credit for his divine intervention.

I still didn't know exactly what happened at that finish line but only knew from another text from Casey that "*it was bad, very bad.*" I didn't know where my mom or sister were but only that when I had left them, their destination was the finish line. Before long, rumors of a bombing were spreading through the streets and were confirmed as we saw bomb squads, helicopters overhead and other special forces racing through the city. Once or twice, a distant boom led us all to believe that other bombs were going off. We felt trapped in the city, thinking that bombs were periodically exploding around us. Many of the runners had left their car keys in their gear bags that were checked into those school buses that took them to the finish line. Those runners felt trapped also, not knowing how or where to get their belongings. Others had planes to catch but their identification was in their bags so they wouldn't have made it through the security check at the airport. Almost all of us needed some sort of public transportation to get out of Boston but it had all been shut down. The presence of tens thousands of confused runners only made the scene more chaotic, but the chaos kept us there, leaving us feeling stuck in a devastating cycle.

At one point, we were told that all runners should go to Boston Common, a central park in downtown Boston, to pick up our gear bags and to meet up with family. Minutes later, we heard that another bomb had been found at the Common. When we saw emergency vehicles speeding towards the Common, we assumed that rumor was true (it wasn't). Many runners were concerned about their loved ones, who should have been at the finish line waiting to cheer them across that famed finish. We were the next wave of runners to finish and it was *our* loved ones who should have been filling the stands and lining the streets of the finish shoot. Exhaustion, disorientation, fear, terror, and concern filled the air and created a tense energy all around us. Yet I stood there, wrapped in a peace that truly surpassed all understanding.

That cheap, pay-by-the-minute phone Casey insisted I carry with me ended up being of great value to me that day. I was so reluctant to carry a phone in the marathon. Before the race started, I couldn't see any good reason for me to have that annoying device with me as I ran the streets of Boston. Casey knew me, my forgetfulness, and especially my tendency to get lost. Because of that, he insisted I carry it. He was always so supportive of me that I carried it for him. That phone not only gave me access to his calls, which brought the news of the bombing- it also gave me a way to find out the fate of my mom and sister. For a short time following the bombing, we were able to send some spotty and delayed texts, learning that although we were separated, we were all safe. We used those text messages to determine our relative locations and within an hour, we were reunited. Despite the fact that it took nearly an hour to reunite, when we found each other we learned that we were never more than a half mile away from one another and were all on the same street the entire time.

I was relieved to learn that the trolley Mom and Amy were on, en route to the finish line, was stopped and the passengers were told to get off. They had never made it to the finish line. Had they taken my advice the night before and gone straight to the finish line until I crossed it, they would have been at the finish line when the bombs went off. I am so thankful that they didn't listen to me.

What the city of Boston needed at that point was for all of the runners and spectators to clear out, leaving officials to focus on the victims and the investigation. Unfortunately, without keys and IDs, and with family and friends separated, many people had no options for leaving. To further complicate matters, all public transportation was shut down and the information coming to the people on the streets was often inaccurate as it spread from person to person. The yellow school buses containing the runners' gear bags were parked inside the police perimeter, so although we could see them, we were not allowed in. After a couple wild goose chases, we gave up on getting my gear bag and focused on getting back to our hotel. We couldn't get transportation back to the train depot, so we walked a long way before finally making it to the South Station. Along the way, we heard that the T was going to resume service.

I distinctly recall the three of us standing on the platform at the station. It was dark and overcrowded. At that moment and in that setting, everyone around us seemed to be suspiciously dressed in dark clothing and carrying black backpacks. There was a heavy law enforcement presence and they all seemed to have automatic weapons. At that moment, being in that tight space, we felt utterly helpless with the bombers still at large. We were aware that there was no way for us to get out if a problem arose. Train after train was full. We were feeling claustrophobic as it became clear we weren't going anywhere anytime soon. Finally, after a long, tense wait, we made it onto a train car and headed back to where Mom and Amy had left the rental car earlier that morning.

Once back at our hotel, we sat in the lobby, exhausted and shocked at the images we were seeing on the news. Though we had been part of the Boston Marathon that day, personally affected by the bombing, and on the outskirts of the tragedy, we had no idea what carnage and loss took place on Boylston Street that day until we saw it on the news. Our physical and emotional weakness suddenly broke with overwhelming grief for our fellow runners and spectators. Like every other American watching the tragic news on television, we felt lumps in our throats, sickness in our stomachs and had no words to express our feelings. Went to bed that night feeling numb.

All three of our flights were scheduled for the next day. We packed up our stuff in silence and headed back to Boston. We heard on the news that morning that gear bags could be picked up in a designated area in downtown Boston. Mom and Amy agreed to drive me back there before heading to the airport. With some serious navigation skills by Mom and Amy, we found the temporary staging area where runners could pick up their belongings. Unable to find parking, they dropped me off and I walked to the pick-up area while they drive around in circles, waiting for me. The race volunteer checked my race number to verify my identity and went to retrieve my bag. He returned with my bag, and to my surprise, he also had a finisher's medal in his hands. He set the bag at my feet and I leaned forward as he ceremoniously placed the medal around my neck. I found myself overwhelmed with emotion and tears broke as I uprighted myself, making eye contact with him. I forced the edges of my lips into a slight smile and mouthed my deeply sincere thanks. With one hand I reached for my bag and with the other, I covered my mouth as I sobbed, surveying the scene around me. An armored vehicle was parked just a few yards from me, television crews were everywhere, and police presence was notable. An ominous feeling weighed heavily on the town and there I stood, blurring the scene with tears, trying to make sense of how this contrasted with the elated feeling a runner gets crossing the finish line, victoriously receiving a finisher's medal.

When I turned to leave the staging area, a television reporter with a cameraman asked if he could interview me. I agreed and he asked what I was feeling at that moment. I didn't exactly know how to put into words the emotions that were whirling inside of me. "This isn't how it's supposed to be," I said as tears rolled down my cheeks.

I returned to the corner where the girls had dropped me off and waited for them to come back. Once in the car, I felt small in the backseat, with a huge medal that I technically didn't earn around my neck and the tall buildings towering overhead. Mom and Amy understood my emotion and we made a quiet drive back to the airport, wrapping up a weekend that played out so differently than the way we had anticipated.

While waiting for my flight to go home, I grabbed a newspaper and shoved it in my carry-on, as updates on the bombing blasted from TV screens at every turn. An internal conflict arose within me. On one hand, I missed my family and wanted to be wrapped in Casey's arms, knowing I was safely back at the secluded camp that we called home. Horses in the front yard and a lake in the back, I knew the rural scenery would be good for me too. On the other hand, I felt like a traitor, leaving Boston in its time of greatest need. They were working around the clock, caring for victims, trying to help displaced runners and, most shockingly, on a manhunt for the two brothers responsible for the terror. I remembered thinking on the day of the bombing that what Boston needed most was for us to all clear out. Yet, I felt a sense of solidarity with the people of Boston and knew that they couldn't just fly away to a rural camp to heal. They had to stay, dealing with the horror of the previous day's events and facing what was to come as the manhunt played out the rest of that week. Though I didn't live there, I felt like I was going AWOL, deserting the people of Boston. Of course, I was never missed in Boston but somehow, I still felt like a deserter. I clasped the medal around my neck as I wiped tears from my eyes and boarded my plane, refocusing on my precious family at home, who was most certainly missing me.

Once back in Georgia I responded to dozens of Facebook posts from people concerned for my well-being. I gave a couple of newspaper interviews as, I'm guessing, local papers all around the country wanted stories from their hometown runners as they returned. I loved on my children and cherished the strong silent hugs from Casey. Mostly, I sat on the front porch swing praying for Boston while facing brilliant sunsets that silhouetted horses in the field. I was surrounded by such a peaceful environment that stood in stark contrast to what was happening in Boston. I prayed that those there would feel the same peace I had felt from the Lord when I stood in the midst of the pandemonium of race day, knowing that peace doesn't come from "what" surrounds us. Peace comes from "Who" is at work in us.

Over time I found healing in quiet prayer time spent on that swing, and through slow, prayer-filled miles run on country roads. I built my mileage back up and grew stronger again, physically too. I soon learned that the Boston Athletic Association had decided to give race entry into the 2014 marathon to those who were unable to finish in 2013 due to the bombings. I was humbled by the gesture and resolved to go back. This time I would truly earn my finisher's medal.

8

Selfless Courage

At the end of May, just six weeks after the bombings in Boston, I was driving through Atlanta with Ester, a dear friend of mine. I had experienced a lot of healing up to that point but the weight of the past few months was heavy upon me.

In February, the same month I had suffered the devastating miscarriage, we had moved to a local camp for inner-city children. Casey hit the ground running in his new position as the facilities director and was immediately overseeing a 20,000 square foot building project in addition to maintaining the other facilities that were on the 300-acre property. Living onsite where we worked meant that Casey was always on call. Wanting to please everyone with whom he worked, he had a hard time establishing boundaries for our family time together, putting a tremendous strain on our marriage. On top of grieving the loss of our unborn child, moving, starting a new ministry and increased marital pressures, I had travelled to Boston in high spirits but had come home with a broken heart over the tragedy that took place there.

"I'm worn out," I lamented to Ester on that Thursday, the day before our last day of school before summer break. "I just don't think I can take anymore right now. I am ready for summer break. I just need time to take it easy and recover from everything, you know? I'm just ready for a relaxing and easy summer."

There was a moment of silence that lasted just long enough for me to let out a deep sigh before my phone rang. It was Casey. He was calling to tell me that one of the leading male counselors at camp wasn't going to be able to come stay at camp for the summer to work because he had become the primary caregiver for his young nephew. The camp director had contacted Casey to ask him if we would be willing to keep the 17-month-old nephew for the summer so the counselor could work.

I wanted to laugh hysterically at the irony of the timing of the call, but I too was deflated and shocked to even breathe. "Let me call you back," my voice cracked. We hung up the phone and I stared out the window of the front passenger door, my eyes darting back and forth, as if searching for something. I *was* searching for something. I was searching for something inside of me to override the self-focused thoughts that were rolling through my brain. *You've been through so much. A miscarriage, a move, a bombing, and your marriage is struggling. You have seven children at home already and are barely keeping your head above water. You don't have the strength for this right now. You. Need. To. Heal.* And then, louder than all those thoughts but somehow gentler, too, I heard the voice of the Lord say, "This isn't about you. This little boy needs your help." I knew it was my Heavenly Father speaking to me because those thoughts weren't mine. My thoughts were all about *me* and *my* needs, but his thoughts were about others and their needs. The entire internal struggle lasted about 30 seconds before I picked up the phone and told Casey, "Yes, we'll do it."

The next day, a stone-faced toddler was dropped off on our front porch. We lived about two hours south of Atlanta and he had ridden the entire way to us on his uncle's lap. Besides an umbrella stroller that his uncle brought, all of his worldly belongings were packed, with room to spare, into a black duffle bag that was handed to us, along with the baby. He came with no instructions. He was a little black boy from the big city who was handed off to a strange white family at a house situated at a rural camp.

"His name is Isaiah," his uncle told us before he kissed his nephew on the cheek and headed off to report to his counselor position. As I turned to go inside with Isaiah in one arm, his duffle bag in another, I was immediately met by a swarm of excited kids. They were all trying to talk to him at once, vying for his attention. Our three-year-old and five-year-old picked up toys to shake in front of his face. Our eight and ten-year-old girls tried tickling his chubby little neck while our 13-year-old son acted out silly antics to make him laugh. Libby, our 11-year-old daughter tried singing to him. Kelsi, our oldest, was on a trip with a friend so we Skyped her to try to entertain Isaiah. None of it worked. Isaiah didn't fuss about being held by complete strangers, but he made no attempts to involve himself with the flurry of well-meaning kids in front of him. He just stared blankly off in the distance. I wondered what he could possibly thinking about his new reality. Later that night, Libby, our blue-eyed songbird, finally got him to sleep by singing to him for what seemed like hours. She was petite and always smaller than other girls her age. He was big for his age with pronounced muscles already. I watched her struggle physically under the load of such a big boy, but she was so loving and patient with him, never giving up on making sure he had a peaceful good night.

That was Memorial Day weekend 2013 and we had a lot of family visiting from out of town. Poor Isaiah, who was already overwhelmed with all the changes and activity around him was bombarded by even more of our family visiting from out of town over the weekend. Through it all, he never smiled and rarely made eye contact with anyone. The only sounds we heard from him were the screams of protest at bath time and his head thrashing in his sleep. After our out-of-town family left, we settled into a new routine with Isaiah and he slowly warmed up to us. Every day we would take him in the stroller to see his uncle working with the camp kids. "Uncle Bro," as he was called by Isaiah, would put on the biggest smile when he saw his nephew "Zay" and we enjoyed observing the connection the two of them shared. Uncle Bro would teach Isaiah to dance and enjoyed showing him off to the other counselors. Anytime Zay was upset or confused, we could ask, "Want to go see Uncle Bro?" and all would be right in his unstable little world.

Isaiah began to enjoy life with the Robinsons. We took him swimming, to pet the horses, and on lots of bike rides around camp. He enjoyed picking blackberries with us and even grew used to all the bugs that came with life in the country. He "helped" me cook, took informal dance lessons from Uncle Bro and found great joy in kicking the basketball around the gym. We marveled at how much he ate, quickly realizing that he could consume his weight in ketchup.

Casey and I were going to marriage counseling weekly throughout the summer, trying to learn how to cope with his increased workload and the added strain of another child in the house. While we loved having Isaiah staying with us, we couldn't see how having a busy toddler added to the mix was God's way of helping us in an already difficult time. We rested in knowing that the Lord's ways weren't our ways and that we had to trust him completely in order to manage the ever-increasing demands each of us were carrying.

Isaiah almost immediately started calling me "Momma" and Casey, "Dad" because that's what he heard from our other kids all day. When he called me Mom, I corrected him and always referred to myself as Ms. Kitty. As much as that stout little toddler was growing on all of us, I often had to be the one to remind myself and the older kids that Isaiah would only be with us for the summer and then he would have to go back. Pretending that I was his mom and he was my son, would only make the separation harder when he had to leave.

One day, while I was carrying Isaiah around camp, an elementary aged African American boy asked me, "Are you his momma?" I laughed inside at the question. I drew my eyebrows together with a distinct questioning look and asked back, "Do I *look* like his momma?" The sweet young man looked at Isaiah, dark skinned with eyes as black night and then at me, freckle faced with 3 layers of SPF 50 on my light skin and then pronounced confidentially, "A little bit." I'll never know what the boy saw in us that could have made us mother and son in his young eyes, but looking back, I have to wonder if that wasn't an example of the Biblical challenge to have "faith like a child."

There were several times over the summer that our kids asked if we could adopt Isaiah. "Isaiah isn't up for adoption," I would tell them. If he was, I couldn't imagine what agency would place him with a family who already had seven children and were living on a missionary's income. The truth was hard, but it was necessary. Isaiah would go home, wherever that was, when the summer was over and that was the end of it. It was out of our hands. God had put him in our life for that short time and we had to trust him that he had a reason, even if we never knew what that reason was. Unfortunately, all the logical thinking in the world couldn't keep us all from falling deeply in love with Isaiah, binding our hearts to his and leaving us to wish he was ours forever.

One night while sitting with Casey at the end of our bed, I held Isaiah in my arms while his chubby brown cheek rested on my shoulder. Drool rolled off his precious lips and soaked into my shirt. "What if he was up for adoption, Casey? Could we be his parents?" I asked him, giving no attention to the fact that I didn't even know Isaiah's birthday. Casey stroked Isaiah's back and answered, "I know how to raise kids, but I don't know if I have what it takes to raise him to be a black man. He may need more than I have to give him." While the words may not sound politically perfect, I understood what he meant. We lived in the deep south. African Americans face a different set of troubles in our society and with racial hatred and police shootings that were dominating the news, we just didn't know. We didn't know how to prepare him for that world, a world that we hadn't reconciled with ourselves. What we knew was that we loved him greatly and that if he ever needed us, that love would have to be enough. It may have been naive to come to that conclusion but that night, cuddling that sweet boy whose future was as unknown to us as his middle name, it seemed to be enough.

As suddenly as Isaiah came into our lives, the summer came to an end and it was time for him to leave. He had spent every moment of those two months with us that summer and had grown close to each member of our family. As much as I tried to protect us all from the pain of the separation that was to come, it turned out that the pain was inevitable. Our hearts were tethered to little Zay in a way that we had no control over. On his last day at Camp Grace, Uncle Bro came to pick up Isaiah. We passed him around and hugged him until he couldn't stand it any longer. The kids were overcome with grief and my heart felt like it was being torn out of my chest as we watched the car carrying Isaiah disappear in the dust from the quarter mile dirt drive that led from our house to the road. We had no idea where he was going or who he would be with for the long term, but we had told his uncle that we were there for Isaiah anytime there was a need.

When each of our other children were babies, we had them dedicated on Baby Dedication Day at church. This was a way that we could publicly declare our commitment to raising our children according to the ways of the Bible. As part of the ceremony, we also acknowledged that our children weren't ours but were basically "on loan" from the Lord. Looking back, it was easy to make that acknowledgement because each baby was safe in our arms when we said it. Every day, our children woke up in our care so how much faith did it really take to say, "They're all yours Lord. We trust you with them"? Isaiah was never *ours* but we felt a parental connection with him that we couldn't allow to be broken when he left us. That day, we had to spiritually place him in the Lord's hands and trust that the Father was protecting him even when he wasn't in our arms or in our home. We found it to be one of the hardest things we had ever done but that transfer of care kept us from fretting over Isaiah's whereabout and level of care. Worrying about his well-being wouldn't help him at all, so we titled ourselves his "Prayer Parents" and added his sweet name to our already long list of our children as we prayed.

The arrival of Isaiah came at such a challenging time and adding the care of a toddler to the mix, left me with little time to deal with the emotional burden that I went into the summer carrying. As much as we enjoyed having Isaiah that summer, he and Emmie, our youngest, spent much of their waking hours in a power struggle that was expressed through ear-piercing screams. Our house was under construction which made it less than ideal for a curious toddler. I was always on my toes and always on call. When Casey and I would try to get away for short walks to reconnect, we were often interrupted by phone calls from building contractors who were vying for Casey's time. We spent 8 weeks with a restless toddler sleeping in a portable crib 2 feet from our bed so that left no space for time alone either. Casey and I were getting away for counseling but the progress we made in a session often felt like it unraveled as soon as we came home to our noisy and rambunctious life.

The stress I entered the summer with wasn't resolved because there never seemed to be time for that. I was blindsided by the task of taking on the care of a toddler and then was hit even harder when he left us. I knew I needed to heal but life was just coming at me so fast. Everywhere I turned, there were responsibilities and the weight of an overwhelming first half of the year was getting hard to stand up under. On the outside, I looked like I was happily juggling it all but, on the inside, I didn't know how much more I could stand without some time to at least catch my breath.

9

Courage to Return

Although marathon training is physically taxing, I was sure the long, lonely training miles would once again be an important part of the recovery my soul was thirsting for. With Isaiah gone and August having already rolled around, I turned my attention back towards Boston. The BAA rarely allowed deferments so their offer of deferrals in light of the bombings was a generous gesture. I planned to make the most of it. I wanted to go back the next year and run in solidarity with others who had been impacted by the terror that was unleashed on the running community and the rest of the country on April 15, 2013. Many people I knew were surprised that I would want to return to Boston, but the Lord gave me the courage and desire to return. In the only way I knew how, I wanted to show terrorists that they couldn't steal our peace.

I knew I had the easy ticket back to the race, but it didn't settle well with me that I didn't earn my way back to the starting line. I didn't like the way I had felt like an outsider in 2013 in Hopkinton at the Athlete's Village. When I would return to stand with Boston in 2014, I didn't want to feel like I didn't belong. I wanted to be Boston Strong. I wrestled with that feeling until I finally decided to run a fall marathon fast enough to re-qualify for the race. Then, when it came time to run the streets of Boston again in 2014, one year after the attack, I could just put one foot in front of the other, experiencing whatever emotions surfaced in that environment and not beat myself up over feeling like I didn't deserve to be there.

Casey and I had finally found a groove within our marriage and our new life at Camp. So with his full support, I set my sights on a November race in Columbus, GA. I had experienced more heart issues during this training cycle but those episodes had become so normal to me that I didn't let them slow me down. Over the years, I had grown accustomed to having to stop on the side of the road to let an episode of chest pain pass. I was used to my heart feeling like it was skipping beats when I exerted myself. I had my heart checked out a couple of times over the years and was given the all clear both times. Those symptoms didn't feel right but the doctors told me what I wanted to hear so I pressed on. By the time the November race weekend rolled around, aside from those unsettling heart issues I had throughout my training, I felt completely ready for the race.

On the morning of the race, we had to get up extra early to give ourselves enough time to make the 2-hour drive to Columbus. As Casey, our ten-year-old daughter Annie, and I left our driveway, Casey told me that he needed to pick something up at my sister Amy's vacation home, which was about 15 minutes from where we lived at Camp Grace.

When we pulled up to my sister's 19th century plantation home, waiting there on the front porch were my brother and his daughter, Bailey. They had made the six-hour drive up from Florida the night before and were ready to drive four more hours round trip that day just to watch me race. This was so characteristic of Chad. He knew how hard I had been training for this race and he knew how much it meant to me to earn my way back in the ranks of other Boston marathoners. Because it meant so much to me, it meant that much to him.

With Casey, Chad, and the girls there to cheer for me, I was ready to take on the Soldier Marathon at Fort Benning. Everything about that day seemed perfect for a fast marathon. I felt well-prepared, and my training had peaked perfectly for the event. The weather was ideal for a strong marathon performance and I had an energetic team cheering me on. I had also run a qualifying marathon on that very course the year before so I knew I could do it. The only dark spot in the day was the feeling that was becoming too familiar at the start of a marathon. With my heart symptoms becoming more regular, I lined up at the start line wondering if I would be one of those people I'd read about in the news that dies while running a marathon. I knew that running just over 8 minutes per mile for 26.2 miles would be even more strenuous than the miles I ran in training and I wondered if my heart could take that kind of stress. Having had good reports from the doctors, I wasn't going to hold back on living my life to the fullest unless I had a diagnosed reason to do so. I pushed the concern out of my mind and lined up ready to give it my all.

For the first 16 miles of the race, I felt strong and swift. *I'm doing it! I'm doing it!* I thought to myself as I stayed on pace with each mile ticked by. "On pace" meant that I would finish in around three and a half hours, matching or bettering my two previous Boston qualifying times of 3:32. Even though I had run those times in the past and had trained hard this time, too, running that fast for that long was never a given. Up to that point, I was pleased with my performance but somewhere in the 17th mile, my legs began to fall flat and lose their strength. I lost over 45 seconds per mile off my pace in those last 9 miles, only finishing the race because a fellow runner named Bob saw me struggling and slowed down to run next to me. He encouraged me to just make it from safety cone to safety cone (which were only about 15 feet apart) and even taking it cone by cone took all the strength I had. I shuffled across the finish line in 3:44:48, which was more than ten minutes over my goal pace and almost 5 minutes over the time needed for my age and gender to qualify for Boston.

Once I recovered from the Columbus Marathon in November, I reassessed my goals. Thinking back on the little pigtailed Kitty that would relentlessly beg her way into front yard football games with the big boys, I knew that she didn't give up easily. Once, when I was a little girl, I begged my dad to take me on an old rickety wooden roller coaster at an amusement park. There was nothing about that roller coaster that looked safe to my dad and given the precious cargo he would entrust to the outdated engineering of the machine, he was completely against the idea. But I had my heart set on riding that roller coaster, so I persisted in asking until my Dad gave in. Putting my big brown eyes and pouty bottom lip to good use, I finally persuaded Daddy to take me on the death trap. Getting in the decrepit car of the roller coaster only made my dad feel worse about the idea but once we got moving, all he could do was hang on and hope for the best. The ride was terrifying! Even at my young age, I could tell it wasn't safe. I screamed in fear the entire ride. My dad said he could see parts that were loose and missing as we flew along the creaking tracks. When the ride finally came to a stop, and my dad had breathed a quick prayer of thanks, I stomped off the roller coaster and refused to speak to him. He pressed and pressed I finally told him why I was so mad, "I can't believe you took me on that horrible ride!" I yelled and then didn't speak to him for the rest of the night.

I was unyielding. And it was that same persistent nature that convinced me to train hard for the 2014 Boston Marathon, where I had already secured deferred entry. With that failed November attempt to run a qualifying marathon before going back to Boston, my new goal was to run a qualifying time while running *in* the Boston Marathon. I would stand with Boston in the first race since the bombing. I would also run a time that proved I belonged. I committed myself to train from November to April to prepare for the Boston Marathon, but as I began yet another cycle of marathon training, my heart symptoms grew worse. I had lived with troubling cardiac warnings for 9 years and had just learned to push through them, but they were getting harder to dismiss.

But one morning during that training cycle, I had to step off the treadmill and slowly lower myself until I was sitting on the side of it. When the discomfort didn't pass, I drove myself home, enduring chest pain the whole way. I had never completely stopped a run due to chest pain before. When I got home, I laid down on the couch for almost 30 minutes until the pain was over. The symptoms were even coming on while I was doing housework or giving one of the little kids a piggyback ride. The problems were creeping into my daily life, and I wasn't comfortable with that. I often warned Casey that if he ever found me unconscious, it was my heart.

I wanted answers but I didn't know what to do to get them. Years before, when we were serving as missionaries in Kentucky, I had a battery of tests done at a local heart center because I was experiencing some of the same symptoms. One of the tests was an echocardiogram. When I had a follow-up appointment with the cardiologists to discuss my results, I couldn't understand much of what he said because his foreign accent was so thick. I heard him say something about mitral valve prolapse, which was a common and usually benign condition, and I clearly heard him say I could still run. That's what I wanted to hear. Armed with a clean bill of health, I filed the test results away and went on with my active life.

Then in 2012, when I was applying for a new life insurance policy, the company requested a copy of that old echo in order to complete my application. A few weeks after submitting the echo results, I received a rejection letter from the life insurance company that stated that, according to the echocardiogram, it was highly likely that I had a terminal heart condition that prevented me from being eligible for coverage. I was stunned. I held in my hand a letter from a life insurance company that basically said I was dying, yet the doctor who performed the test let me walk out of his office without even making a follow-up visit. Something didn't add up. Of course, the first thing I did was Google the condition listed on the rejection letter: pulmonary hypertension. What I found was discouraging.

That Google search scenario closely mirrored the time I first looked up Chiari Malformation. That Google search scenario closely mirrored the time I first looked up Chiari Malformation. This time however, instead of those disturbing words "brain surgery", it would be the equally dreadful "heart surgery." I found myself reading about a rare heart condition that would require a heart and lung transplant for survival. I wanted so badly to disassociate myself from it, but my experience with Chiari suggested otherwise. It too was a rare condition, but sadly, patients usually only lived 3 years after diagnosis. But if I had the condition than I should have already been dead or, at the very least, suffering from degenerative symptoms that were significantly more severe than those that I was experiencing. I wrestled with the facts and the unknown and tried to make them fit together to give me a picture of what was going on with my heart, but I just couldn't reconcile the details.

I had to get answers for my own peace of mind. I also needed them for my future chances at getting life insurance coverage. If a person is ever turned down for life insurance, it follows them for the rest of their lives. To get answers and to avoid being forever blacklisted from getting life insurance, I was given the option of having another echocardiogram done within 30 days that showed that I was not in the high-risk category for that grave heart condition. That seemingly easy option was complicated by the fact that I didn't even have health insurance and I didn't have money to pay for the test. Through a connection at Camp Grace, we found a doctor who offered to do the echo free of charge. Even though I had to wait two weeks for the appointment, I was relieved that I was going to finally get some answers.

Waiting for that 2012 appointment ended up being pivotal in my faith. I had been given horrible and confusing news by the insurance company and there was no way to reconcile it until I went in for that appointment. In the meantime, I had to come to terms with some crucial thoughts. I had to decide if I would spend the next 14 days in worry and fear, losing sleep and more importantly, peace, over something that was out of my control. Or I had to choose to trust the Lord. Matthew 6:27 says that we cannot add a single day to our lives by worrying. Not only was I not able to add days to my life through worrying, I would lose two good weeks of peaceful family time if I chose to spend them in fear.

I chose faith and to work on doing what the Bible calls, "taking every thought captive," meaning that as negative thoughts crept in, I would put them out of my mind and replace them with healthy and positive thoughts. This practice helped me to thrive in that time of uncertainty instead of crumbling. I did however, use that time to reflect on how I was living my life. What if my time was more limited than I had thought? What if I wouldn't see my children grow up? How would I do things differently? I truly believe that everyone should "live like you were dying" as Tim McGraw sings about in his song. The Lord used that time to help me prioritize my life and to help me remember what matters most.

The day finally came for my appointment. I had the echo done and then the doctor came in to discuss the results with Casey and me. Casey squeezed my hand as the doctor sat down, looking over the printout. He held such life-altering information in his hands so the time it took him to give us the news seemed to drag on.

Looking up from the paper in his hands, he said, "You do not have pulmonary hypertension." I let out a deep, sigh of relief and he went on. "You have a bit of prolapse in your mitral valve but I don't think that will be an issue for you. You also have mild regurgitation in your bicuspid valve but, again, it's not a big deal." What a relief that news was! Since I had a free appointment with a cardiologist, I started to ask him about my symptoms and the problems I had been having when I was exerting myself just to be sure I was clear to keep up my running. He interrupted me before he had the chance to hear about the heart problems I'd been having. "You're fine. Look at you. You're young and healthy. Go run marathons! Oh, and come back in a year and I'll check you again for free." I turned his report into the insurance company and put the ordeal behind me, thankful for the spiritual life lessons that were wrapped up in it all.

I wasn't looking for a problem and only wanted to know that I could live my life to the fullest. So the doc's encouragement to keep running was exactly I wanted to hear. If standing by the side of the road, with my hand clenching my chest in pain was acceptable and "normal" to the heart doctor, then I would continue to live with it. After that appointment in 2012, I reconciled that as long as I knew I wasn't risking leaving my family without a mother and that I could run, I was happy with the news.

However, in 2013, after that episode of chest pain on the treadmill, I decided to take the heart doctor's offer to come back for an annual check-up. It had been over a year since the echo results that freed me from the life insurance nightmare, so I called and made an appointment. That 30-minute chest pain scare was severe enough for me to suspend my running until I was checked out again. Although I went back to the same cardiologist group, I didn't get an appointment with the doctor that time. I had an echocardiogram done by a technician and received a call a week later from a nurse telling me that my results were fine.

But I was still having severe episodes of chest pain and frequent palpitations. I was getting worse but I felt there was nothing I could do about it. Over the last eight years, I'd had two doctors perform three echocardiograms on me and all gave me a clean bill of health. To go back to the doctor again would, in my mind, put me in the category of a hypochondriac. One night, while at dinner in the camp cafeteria, I began having chest pain. That was one of the only times that I can remember having problems with my heart while at rest. I was sitting at a round table that was filled with my sweet children and I didn't want them to know I was having a problem. I bowed my head down and took a few deep, quiet breaths, waiting for the episode to pass. It didn't. Until that day, I had been able to keep the problems I was having with my heart basically under wraps. Casey knew about it and maybe a couple friends did because of the tests I'd had over the years, but other than that, I was able to keep whatever "it" was private. That night, Casey was working with the camp kids and couldn't be pulled away. I was feeling pretty bad and needed help getting myself and our children back to our house. I hated the predicament I found myself in. I didn't like to draw that sort of attention to myself, but I needed help. I quietly explained to Susie, our camp founder's wife, what was going on and she sweetly took charge of my children and gave me a golf cart ride home. After making sure I was tucked in bed, she started asking me questions and my answers sounded ignorant. It sounded insane that I was living with such severe heart symptoms yet was doing nothing about it. This was why I didn't tell many people about it! I just didn't want to be one of "those people" who ran to the doctor every time they sneezed. I had been to the doctor three times about my heart and each time was told the same thing. On top of that, I didn't have health insurance either. I didn't know what else I could do.

My reality, though, was that the symptoms were creeping into every area of my life, to the point that they interrupted my time with my family and finally had me concerned enough for me to pause my running again. My quality of life was suffering. When I went to bed that night that Susie took me home, I wondered if I would wake up in the morning. This was no way to live.

I felt fine the next morning. A few days later, I came up with a new explanation for my heart problems. Maybe everything was fine with my heart and perhaps my brain was growing compressed again after so many years since my brain surgery. This was an unfortunate possibility with Chiari and would require another decompression surgery. The lowest part of the brainstem, the medulla, is the most vital part of the brain and controls the heart and lungs. As much as I didn't want to face more issues with Chiari, I felt a sense of relief at the thought of having a possible explanation for what I was experiencing.

I called my heart doctor's office and ordered the results of that third echocardiogram (which I had never actually seen). When I received it, I became aware that for the third time in three echocardiograms, my numbers were in the high-risk category for pulmonary hypertension. Between that and the Chiari theory, I was armed and ready to take my case to a doctor. I recalled from a previous appointment that one of the heart doctors' in my group was female. I had male doctors who just didn't take their time with me and had this strong sense that a woman would listen to me. I made an appointment with Dr. Amy Kingman and held off on running again until I met with her.

When Dr. Kingman entered the examining room that morning in February of 2014, I immediately noticed that she was physically fit which made me feel that she would care about how the problems that I had while running were affecting me. When I started to share my symptoms with her, she didn't interrupt and send me on my way like the men had done. Instead, she listened, like a girlfriend would. I explained my theory of Chiari being the possible cause and then I showed her the results to all three of my echocardiograms, feeling that this was my last attempt at getting to the bottom of this. She agreed that it was time for answers and the only way to get an accurate reading of the pressure between my heart and lungs to rule out pulmonary hypertension was to do a heart catheterization. A heart cath is an invasive imaging procedure where a catheter is threaded up through a vein in the leg and routed to the heart to give doctors accurate evaluations on pressures and blockages. I was so encouraged that I would finally get a definitive test done. But my heart almost stopped when I learned the test can cost upwards of $20,000 and I didn't have health insurance. In faith, I made the appointment to have the cath done and went to work on getting insurance to cover what would now be considered a preexisting condition.

Thanks to the Affordable Care Act, I was able to get insurance with my potentially preexisting condition. But also thanks to the ACA, the process was difficult and ended up being the only circumstance in all of this unpredictable heart story that brought me to tears. The 'Affordable Care' was also very expensive and we didn't make enough money to qualify for a subsidy. We had to make more money in order to qualify for the government to subsidize our healthcare. We also made too much to get help from Medicaid, so we fell into some sort of grey area where there was no help. I didn't believe it was the government's job to help pay for my healthcare anyway but knowing that those options were part of the plan that was rolled out for Americans, yet I was unable to tap into them was disappointing. My oldest sister, Beth, found out about my troubles with getting healthcare and insisted on "subsidizing" me herself. As a successful single working woman, she had the expendable income to help me in my time of need and she was more than willing. Every month, for nearly a year, she sent me a handwritten card with a check that covered my healthcare premium. It was amazing to see the Lord provide through her and she was blessed to be used by him. With insurance in place, and the appointment made with the hospital for the heart cath, I was ready to get the answers I'd been waiting for.

10

The Fight for Courage

Dr. Kingman wasn't able to perform my heart cath because my mild tricuspid valve regurgitation made the procedure a little trickier than normal. She scheduled one of her colleagues to do the procedure that day and I met him briefly before they took me back to the cath lab. My long-time friends, Celia and Milinda, had driven up from Florida to stay with the children so Casey could be with me at the hospital. The catheterization seemed to go smoothly, although I noticed my heart go into a funny rhythm when they probed one area. The catheter is inserted into the patient's groin and once removed, the area has to be given constant, firm pressure for 15 minutes. Having a nurse stand over me to apply very firm pressure for that long was the worst part of the procedure for me. I closed my eyes and focused on other things and took myself to other places while I waited for the time to go by. When the nurse was finally done, the doctor came in to review my results. Casey and I had no idea what he was going to tell us but we did know that that test would be the final determinant as to whether or not I had pulmonary hypertension which would have been an extremely grave diagnosis.

The doctor smiled as he told us that the pressures between my heart and lungs were completely normal. We were so relieved to finally hear that! From then on, the echocardiogram readings didn't matter. The heart cath result had the final say and we were overjoyed with the conclusion. Hearing that I didn't have pulmonary hypertension was definitely what I wanted to hear but I had gone through the risk, discomfort, and expense of a heart cath to find out what *was* wrong with my heart. With pulmonary hypertension ruled out, I didn't know what the next step was in determining the source of my symptoms. My answer came when the doctor said, "Oh, there was one artery that I couldn't find to probe, so you'll need to follow up with Dr. Kingman on that. She will probably have you do a CT scan to check on that but I'm sure it's nothing." A missing artery surely didn't sound like "nothing" to us but once again, we would have to wait to get the answers we needed.

When enough recovery time had passed since the heart cath, I got up to head home from the outpatient procedure. As I tried to stand up, my blood pressure bottomed out and Casey and the nurse got me back in bed just in time to keep me from passing out. This little scene played out several more times before the medical staff decided to keep me overnight. With my Florida friends at home with the kids, Casey was able to stay with me, giving us the first night away together we had in a long time! While we were at the hospital, one of the kids had thrown up and we didn't know if it was an isolated incident or the start of a stomach bug. When I was released the next day, Casey and I decided that it would be best if I didn't go home for a few days because any extreme pressure from coughing, lifting or vomiting could cause the entrance wound to pop open, leaving me at risk for severe bleeding. Two of our sweet friends from church, Larry and Bobby Hines, who lived close to the hospital, let me stay at their house so I could spend the next couple of days recovering in the peaceful environment of their home.

While at their house, I pulled out my paperwork from the hospital and read through it. The results from the heart cath said that I had an anomalous right coronary artery. So that was the "missing artery." Once again, I went to the web (reliable medical sites only, of course) to find out what I could about the right coronary artery (RCA). I learned that the RCA supplies blood to the right side of the heart. It originates from the lower side of the aorta and then feeds the heart. So, if mine wasn't where it was supposed to be, where was it? And would it need to be fixed? I read on to learn that sometimes an RCA could be in the wrong place, but it didn't necessarily mean it was causing problems. However, less commonly, an anomalous RCA was coming out from in between two other vessels, the aorta and pulmonary artery, and getting compressed by those vessels during exertion. Anomalous coronary arteries were the cause of 15% of sudden death in athletes and out of those deaths, 80% of the victims had arteries that ran between the two vessels. Basically, when I had heard of young athletes dying suddenly on the track or the basketball court, many of them had the same anomaly that I was born with. All those times that I lined up at the starting line of a marathon, I had every reason to feel as though I could be one of those runners who I read about dying along the course.

I learned from my "research" on the Internet that if my RCA was just a little out of place, no treatment would be needed but I would back to square one in figuring out the source of my troubling heart symptoms. If the RCA was originating between the aorta and pulmonary artery, then it would have to be moved. As I sat in the Hines' living room, them watching TV and me with my laptop and hospital discharge papers scattered around me, my thoughts went back to that young girl who grew up running everywhere: running watermelons to the bus stop, running home from school and later running several tough seasons of track and cross country. Had that young girl done all that running on a heart with a potentially fatal defect? And was the running the very activity that could have triggered sudden death? Then I started to think about my life more recently. I had run many 5k races, a couple half marathons and seven marathons and I prepped for each of those races with countless miles out on the roads alone. Surely, if my RCA was in a precarious position, I would have known by then.

My mind went back and forth between the two possibilities, taking into consideration my symptoms. Once again, I found myself in the position where I had to decide how I was going to handle the unknown. Would I spend the time between that night and the day I would receive my CT results in turmoil, constantly thinking of the possibilities? Or would I choose to give the situation to the Lord, knowing that it was out of my control? I chose to trust. I asked the Lord to give me the courage to wait patiently and peacefully. I didn't need the courage to face surgery that night. I only needed to the courage each day to trust the Lord with my future. Knowing that he had always been faithful, this was the path I chose.

When the day of the CT scan came, I was pleased to be attended to by a precious nurse who seemed genuinely interested in my life and my care. She was experienced, friendly and inspiring and I enjoyed her company. She alone did all the necessary preparations for the test, making me feel at ease knowing I was in her hands. As she wheeled me down to the imaging room, she asked about my family and, like everyone else, was shocked to learn that I had seven children, had undergone brain surgery and was at the Boston Bombing. My life story *was* a surprise to so many people, but it was just as much of a surprise to me as each of those events unfolded over the years!

The CT scan didn't go as smoothly as I had expected. The nurse had placed an IV in my arm through which the technicians pushed a specialized dye into my bloodstream. At certain points in the scan I was instructed to hold my breath so the technicians could get clear images but when the dye raced into my heart, my heart started to beat erratically, making it difficult for clear images to be recorded. The nurse went into the imaging area to join the technicians and help them determine if they obtained the images they needed or if they would have to try again. They all whispered among themselves as I lay on the table, awaiting further instructions. They weren't happy with the images. After several more tries, the IV coming loose from my arm and more episodes of my heart racing in response to the dye, they still weren't 100% sure that they got the pictures they needed. Those images, they decided, were the best they could get, given my heart's unsettling response to the procedure.

When the nurse came out of the imaging area to help unhook me from the medical equipment and get me back into the wheelchair, her countenance was clearly different. The same lady that I felt such a connection with looked at me differently and seemed guarded. I couldn't shake the look the nurse gave me as she wheeled me out of the CT scan. It was a look of empathy and seemed to say, "I'm so sorry for what you're about to face." I also couldn't forget how my heart reacted when the IV medicine given during the scan surged through my veins and passed through my heart. It palpitated so fast that I didn't know what to make of it.

The next day, my doctor's office called. "Dr. Kingman needs to see you regarding the results of your scan," the lady from the office told me. I was confused. I had already made a follow up appointment with her for later that week. When I told the receptionist that, she told me I could just keep my original appointment. As I hung up the phone, I found I had another puzzling piece of information to add to my burdened mind. Up to that point, I had such peace about everything but with that one phone call, I became unglued inside. The courage that I sought from the Lord to get me to that test seemed to be fading. Instead of fighting for peace, I allowed myself to struggle greatly with all the unknowns.

Questions about the unknown were overpowering my peaceful mind. Why did the doctor's office call me so soon after my scan? Why did she need to make an appointment right away? Wouldn't they only call me to schedule an appointment to go over the results if it was bad news? Why did the nurse look at me that way? What were her sad blue eyes trying to tell me? Why couldn't my heart handle the CT scan medicine as it pumped it through my body? Why was I having the symptoms that brought me to the point of needing all these tests anyway?

Instead of facing these unanswered questions with peace, I allowed those thoughts to consume me. They gnawed at my stomach and weighed heavily on my heart. I decided to call the cardiologist's office back to ask if they could tell me my results over the phone. After all, they were *my* results. If the doctors knew knew, I should know, too! But I ran into a brick wall in my effort to get the results over the phone.

That night I couldn't get to sleep. As I lay in the dark with my head on my pillow in my safe and comfortable room, I wondered what was in store for me as more questions haunted me. Was I about to face open heart surgery? Was I going to be temporarily trading my familiar bedroom with a stale, unwelcoming ICU room? What was wrong with me? Why did someone else have that answer... someone who's probably sleeping soundly with the results while I was frozen in fear wanting to know? I physically couldn't stand knowing that someone else knew and I didn't. It was too much.

I eventually fell into an unsettled sleep and woke up the next morning feeling frozen by fear of the unknown. Like a robot, I went through my morning routine of getting ready for the day, but I was absorbed with wondering if I would have my breast bone cut apart, my heart stopped and repaired, forever leaving me with a giant scar down the middle of my chest. I allowed my mind to dwell on those same corrosive questions all day, playing them over and over in my mind like a broken record. Why did the doctor's office call? Why did the nurse look at me like that? Why couldn't my heart handle that test? What was I about to walk through? Those same questions repeated in my mind until I felt sick and was shaking.

I knew I couldn't spend even just the three days waiting until my follow up appointment in the same anxious state I had suddenly found myself in. I had to get to the root of those feelings and get them out of my heart. After much soul searching, I realized that I wasn't fearful of the outcome. Instead, I was bothered by the wait. I didn't like that the doctor knew my results and I didn't. I wanted to know my "fate" right away. This impatience manifested itself in me in the form of constant internal turmoil. I woke up thinking about it, went to bed thinking about it and struggled with those thoughts all day.

This was so out of character for me. When I went through brain surgery almost a decade before, I was filled with the peace that passes all understanding. In every difficult situation along the way the Lord gave just what I needed, when I needed it. This current anxiety became an all-consuming struggle for me. I was reminded of a story I heard from Pastor Francis Chan where he talked of a church member who was a former Mr. Universe. His wife was also a bodybuilder and together, they were quite an impressive pair. Anyone would expect that that couple's children would be strong and tough, too. But what if, he mused, they were the weak, little twerps. Then he made the connection between that scenario and the Lord.

We serve a mighty and powerful God who is capable of *anything*. Why then do so many Christians walk around fearful and anxious when we're *his* children? It just doesn't add up! Our Father in heaven is a mighty God so we should live with a mighty faith. Because of this, I could not accept anxiety as a "normal" emotion given my circumstance. God promises peace in *all* situations, so I began to plead to the Lord to help me through the anxious and impatient feelings I was having and to replace them with peace.

No matter how hard I prayed, and how much scripture I read, I couldn't shake the anxiety. I felt so strongly that no matter what I would have to face in regard to my health that I wanted to look back and know I pleased my Heavenly Father with how I handled it. So I prayed even more. I pleaded with the Lord to give me a word or something that would ease my heart and mind. Later that afternoon, Carla, a good friend of mine came to visit. When she heard that I was having tests done on my heart, she offered to pray for me as we walked around camp. She had no idea of the inner turmoil I was facing. But as she prayed for me, she said, "And I thank you Lord that you already know..."

With those words and the realization that God already knew the results, I was filled with peace... a peace that washed away the anxious feelings. It was so elementary, but that was the word from God that I had prayed for earlier. It was just the reminder I needed. I didn't need to know my results right away because God already knew them. God was so faithful to have answered my prayer.

Around this same time, we had heard through some camp staff that Isaiah was displaced again, this time living with his grandmother. We hadn't seen Isaiah since he left us at the end of July and hadn't heard from him or Uncle Bro since about two weeks after they left camp. Casey and I had continued to pray for him diligently and the kids often asked about him. Over the months since he left, I had several similar dreams of him being with us again. In each dream, he was brought to us- basically given to us. In one dream in particular, we were in our van stopped at a red light when a truck pulled up next to us. Uncle Bro popped out of the truck and came towards me with Isaiah in his arms, as I sat in the front passenger seat. I threw the door open and Uncle Bro placed Zay into my arms. I scooped him up onto my lap and held him tight. Uncle Bro smiled and said with great joy, "He's yours!"

I don't remember the details of all the dreams except that Isaiah was always brought to us in them. I do remember rubbing my cheek on his in each dream, smelling his skin and trying to make the moment last before I woke up. When I would awake, my arms would be empty, and Isaiah may as well have been a million miles away. When the kids heard about Isaiah's current situation, they all asked if we could adopt him. It seemed like the perfect opportunity to pursue him, but with the uncertainty of my heart diagnosis, Casey and I agreed that we would wait until we were on the other side of the heart situation before we would pursue Isaiah.

The day of my follow up appointment with Dr. Kingman finally came, and I went into the day of my appointment with true peace. As I was getting ready to leave the house, the receptionists called to tell me that my doctor had the flu and couldn't see me until the next day. Amazingly, I didn't even feel upset for a moment because I recognized the circumstance as a test to see if I was only willing trust the Lord for a certain amount of time. With my appointment another 24 hours away, I had to choose to fully walk in the faith I had been given.

I slept peacefully that night, knowing that whatever I was about to face was in the Lord's hands. I found out the next day that Dr. Kingman was still ill and wouldn't be able to see me. They scheduled me with the heart doctor who did my cath. As much as I loved Dr. Kingman and knew she was the only cardiologist who ever really listened to me, I surmised that I wouldn't need this other doctor to listen to me- he would only be giving me test results.

Casey and I walked into the cardiologist's office surrounded by a cloud of peace. We sat down with the doctor whom I'd only met briefly before and after my heart cath. He was the guy who told me he was sure the missing artery was nothing but that I would need the CT scan. Now in his office, he looked over my CT findings and got out a blank piece of paper and a pen. He began to draw a rough sketch of what the heart looks like and said, as he drew, "This is where your right coronary artery is supposed to be and…" I took a deep breath as I leaned in to see where his pen would move to next on the drawing. This was the answer I needed. I was about to find out if my RCA was in a safe place or if it originated between two vessels that were compressing it. "*Your* right coronary artery, however, is originating from in between these two great vessels," he pointed to each and named them for me. I couldn't believe it. I had the exact condition that I had read about that night as I recovered on the Hines' couch. It was the rare condition that caused sudden death in athletes and the only way to fix it was open heart surgery. I focused back into what the doctor was saying as he continued, "but people can live with this and given your symptoms, I think you'll be fine. Just come back in a year for follow up."

I was shocked by the nonchalant way he gave me my diagnosis and tried to send me on my way. Since I had never had an appointment with him before, I asked him if I could tell him my symptoms to make sure he felt that my condition didn't need repair.

"I've heard your symptoms.," he interrupted flatly. I couldn't believe what I had just heard. After years of chest pain, irregular rhythms, palpitations, and concern that my heart could stop at any moment, this guy was going to let me walk out of his office and encourage me to continue to run marathons without even hearing from me! I wasn't going to let him cut me off like that and send me away without understanding the full scale of the problems I'd been having. I didn't *want* to have heart surgery, but I certainly didn't want to walk out of yet another doctor's office without answers. If I had learned anything on this journey, it was that I had to take responsibility for my own healthcare.

"No, you haven't," I answered firmly, feeling more courageous as I went on. "I have never had an office appointment with you. So while I'm here, I would like for you to know what I've been dealing with." He sat back, surprised, and finally looking like he was ready to hear me out. I went on to tell him of the times I had found myself bent over on the side of the road, waiting for chest pain to pass. I told him about all the symptoms I'd had while running, and more recently, even just cleaning or doing less strenuous tasks. I let him know that anytime I had a rush of adrenaline, like before I had to speak publicly or those times when I had a near fender bender, my heart felt overwhelmed as if it couldn't take it. And I got more personal, letting him know that I often had troubling episodes during intercourse with my husband.

As I spoke, his eyes widened with concern and he reached for a pad and began to write out a referral to a heart surgeon.

"I'm sorry but you need heart surgery. You must have this fixed," he said as he handed me the referral. I didn't want heart surgery but more than that, I didn't want to leave that appointment without knowing that the doctor had the full understanding of my history. I needed to know that his decision was based off my reality and not off his desire to hurry through an appointment. If I hadn't stood up to him, insisting that he hear me out, at best I would still be suffering from symptoms that inhibit my quality of life. At worse, I would be dead.

We left the office thankful that I pressed the doctor to take time to listen to me, but in total shock that I would most likely be having open heart surgery. Walking out of the cardiologist's office hand-in-hand, the scenario was eerily familiar to Casey and me. We had just found out that I needed another major surgery on a major organ for a congenital defect. Both my Chiari and my misplaced artery were conditions that didn't manifest themselves until adulthood. I had lived an active childhood in perfect health with only one trip to a doctor for an ear infection and one trip for a hairline fracture.

Yes, my brain and heart were affected by hauntingly similar problems but there were also positive similarities. Both of those conditions were found before any irreparable problems occurred (you know, like, sudden death) and they were both treatable. The most encouraging parallels between the two diagnoses and surgeries was that I didn't have to face any of it alone. I had a Heavenly Father who loved me and was active in providing for me and my family. I had a church family who would support us and a biological family who would rally around me again as they had done when I had brain surgery nearly a decade before. On top of all that, I had a man who cared for me more deeply than any human being ever could and was fully committed to me. Through sickness and health, I knew everything was going to be just fine.

11

Sometimes Courage

When I walked into the examining room, Dr. Joe Johnson was surprised. "You certainly don't look like my typical heart patient!" he exclaimed. I shrugged, acknowledging the obvious. I was used to feeling out of place in cardiologists' offices. One time, as I sat reading a magazine in Dr. Kingman's office, the receptionists called across the room to get my attention. The funny thing was, she didn't use my name like they always have. She just called out, "Ma'am? Ma'am." *Me?* I asked with my eyes. She then pointed to a side door. "You can go on to the back, now." I looked towards the door to the "back" but there wasn't a nurse waiting for me. Normally the nurse would have been standing there, holding my chart and would have called me herself, by my name. I guess the way I folded my magazine, stood up and just stood there with a clueless look on my face prompted the receptionist to repeat herself. When I didn't budge, she finally asked, "You are the pharmaceutical rep., aren't you?" I shook my head no and a well-dressed gentleman further back and out of the receptionists' sight stood up and acknowledged himself as the rep. Of course, they would mistake me for the rep. Everyone else there (besides the actual rep, whom she couldn't see) had grey hair, was 30 years my senior and was thirty or more pounds overweight. I certainly didn't fit the profile when it came to heart patients!

Dr. Johnson was good looking and sharp. He seemed friendly enough- at first. He looked over my chart and asked me to describe my symptoms. I did and he agreed that he would have to do surgery. He began to discuss the details of the surgery with such ease that you would have thought he was just going to be filling a tooth. His familiarity came across as arrogance to the point that I wasn't sure if I liked him or not. I asked him how he would work on my heart while it was pumping. He said it wouldn't be pumping. My eyes widened. He would reroute my blood supply to a machine that would take over the pumping while he uprooted and re-implanted the artery. I began to ask him another question and he quipped, "I'll tell you if you'll just be quiet for a moment and let me talk." Whoa, I didn't know how to react. I was offended but I would be trusting my life in this man's hands, so he was the last person I wanted to have on my bad side. I stepped back and listened while he, like the other doctor, drew an elementary drawing of the heart so that I could easily understand his explanation. I was offended by this seemingly arrogant doctor who had at first appeared to be so friendly.

When he was done explaining the procedure, Dr. Johnson walked Casey and me to his scheduling office and booked the surgery for just a few weeks away. Before he left, I asked Dr. Johnson if my bare chest would be exposed to everyone in the operating room. "Yes, of course," he answered. I firmly told him that I wasn't comfortable with that. After letting me know that my entire body had to be sanitized because my chest cavity would be opened up, I still wasn't satisfied. He reminded me that I would be asleep so it shouldn't bother me. Nope, still not good enough. Just as I sensed that I was getting on his nerves again, he walked me back to the scheduler's office and said to the woman behind the desk, "Please schedule an all-female prep staff for Mrs. Robinson's surgery." She agreed, I was pleased and decided that maybe Dr. Joe Johnson wasn't so bad after all.

Surgery was scheduled for April 7, 2014, exactly one week before the Boston marathon. I had already stopped my marathon training and had to come to terms with the fact that I wasn't going to back to Boston that year. When all of Boston would be standing in unity at the race that year, I would be running a different kind of race, making strides each day towards recovery. The Boston Marathon doesn't grant medical deferments so, if I ever wanted to go back to Boston and take those last two turns that I missed in 2013, I would have to rebuild my mileage and fitness after having heart surgery and regain the speed needed to requalify. But now that I was facing open heart surgery, the possibility of ever being a marathoner again, let alone a Boston qualifier, seemed so far removed.

Once I dealt with the disappointment of knowing my Boston dreams were gone, or at least on hold, I had no difficulty focusing on planning for the surgery ahead. Exactly how big the scar was going to be was something I had to know right away. I sat down and Googled "open heart surgery scar." What came up on the screen shocked me and it became real… I was going to have one of those huge scars going from the bottom of my throat to the bottom of my sternum. It made sense: in order to get to the heart, the rib cage had to be cut open and laid apart and then brought back together, leaving that infamous scar. What was crazy was that the open heart surgery scar wouldn't be my first scar of that size. I had another scar- just as serious of a scar and just as big- already on the back of my head. We saw it for a time when my hair was shaved off and the 19 stitches held together my healing flesh. In time, the stitches were removed, and my hair grew out. Now, all those years later, there was just a little bit of the line showing at the back of my neck. Since I wore my hair long, the only ones that ever saw that scar were my children. When they played with my hair, the first thing they did was to part my hair and go looking for the bottom of my scar and we would talk of God's faithfulness. Maybe that's how it would be with the new scar except it would be visible by so many. Perhaps every time somebody saw it, I would have the opportunity to talk of God's faithfulness. Was it possible that my scars would be, in a very small way, like the 12 stones set in the Jordan by Joshua in the Bible, put there as a remembrance of God's deliverance, his faithfulness?

I spent more time learning what I should expect from the surgery and recovery, growing thankful for people who shared their photos and stories online. I had known several older people who had endured OHS and knew what their recoveries were like. I wondered, though, what recovery would be like for a runner who's in her thirties. I wondered how long it would take for me to return to *my* normal level of activity. One day, I found a blog written by the mother of a teenage girl who had OHS to repair an anomalous RCA. The daughter was a sports enthusiast who played soccer and ran cross country. It was after a cross country meet that she started having chest pain and was taken to the emergency room. After some tests, they discovered the problem and she soon had the same surgery I was facing. What amazed me about her story is that she was back to competing in soccer just 6 weeks after her surgery! Her first couple of weeks post-op involved short and very slow recovery walks. She was discouraged that it took her around 30 minutes just to walk a half mile. From there though, her healing began progressing rapidly. Within a month and a half, with the doctor's permission, she had rejoined her team on the soccer field. That story motivated me more than anything else I read. Even though I was older than the girl I read about, I decided that my recovery would be more like hers than anyone else I had seen. I would stay positive and quickly get back to doing the activities I loved.

I got to see my actual heart doctor, Dr. Kingman, one last time before surgery. While she conducted a treadmill stress test, we were able to discuss how I had been feeling emotionally in light of my diagnosis. I told her that I was just happy to have an explanation for how my heart had been reacting for so many years. Our conversation led to me sharing with her how bad my heart was during my pregnancy with Emmie, my seventh baby. Dr. Kingman said that she wasn't sure I would have survived the eighth pregnancy that ended in miscarriage. Losing that baby devastated me but hearing that from Dr. Kingman helped ease the pain a bit. I have never valued my life over the life of my unborn child but somehow it still made the loss easier to bear.

As my surgery date grew closer, I had people asking me if I was getting nervous or suggesting to me that I must be nervous. There were tears in people's eyes as they hugged me, telling me they hoped the surgery would go well. I went through the same experience before brain surgery years ago. There was something behind those words, those tears, and those hugs. It was as if loved ones weren't sure if it would be their last interaction with me, so they clung a little tighter. I genuinely appreciated their thoughts and their intentions, but once again, there was fear in their voices, and I had to stay far from that. The Lord had given me peace that would pass all understanding and I didn't want fear to sabotage that.

On the Wednesday night before heart surgery, I was hearing a lot of these comments. I was in line at family night supper at church, scooping mashed potatoes onto my plate when a fellow church member made eye contact with me and said, "I bet you're getting nervous, aren't you?" I confidently told her that I was feeling peaceful about the upcoming surgery and moved onto putting roast beef and gravy over my potatoes. By the time I made it to the green beans, another fear-filled comment came my way. "Only a few more days until your big surgery, huh? I'm sure you're feeling pretty anxious about it." But I wasn't. I didn't choose to follow the One who created everything, including my heart, just to turn from trusting him when a trial came my way. As I walked from church supper to the sanctuary for prayer meeting, I started to wonder why I felt so confident if everyone around me expected me to be nervous and anxious. Was I being ignorant? Was there something I was supposed to be afraid of? Did I not see the whole picture?

The answer to those questions seemed to come straight from the Lord. Without even having to consciously think about it, my lips started to audibly recite Psalm 121. This is a chapter from the Bible that I had memorized with my kids years earlier. To be honest, I hadn't thought of the verse in a very long time, yet it was welling up from my heart and rolling off my tongue as if I had just learned it the week before.

"I lift up my eyes to the mountains—

where does my help come from?

My help comes from the Lord,

the Maker of heaven and earth.

He will not let your foot slip—

he who watches over you will not slumber;

indeed, he who watches over Israel

will neither slumber nor sleep.

The Lord watches over you—

the Lord is your shade at your right hand;

the sun will not harm you by day,

nor the moon by night.

The Lord will keep you from all harm—

he will watch over your life;

the Lord will watch over your coming and going

both now and forevermore."

The Lord used those verses to remind me why I had such peace and confidence. I could face surgery, or anything in life, because my help came from the Lord! My confidence was in him and the peace that I felt came from him. That experience made me so thankful that I had taken the time to memorize scripture and solidified the value of learning it. I needed it that day and am so thankful that though I wasn't consciously thinking of it, it was there to comfort me when I needed it the most.

I was enveloped with peace in those weeks leading up to the surgery. But one night, I woke up suddenly from a dream and sat straight up in bed, covered in sweat. I took a couple of deep breaths and closed my eyes to reflect on the dream. In my dream, doctors were opening my chest cavity to begin the repair to my heart. But when the heart became visible to them, they could see all the sinful thoughts of my heart, spiritually speaking. My subconscious mind had taken the spiritual matters of the heart and replaced the physical heart with them. In the dream, the doctors could visibly see all of my inadequacies. They could see every offense that I'd ever committed. A lifetime of mess ups, known and unknown, were suddenly public. Words like *liar* and *thief* were scribbled on my heart, fighting for space and covering the entire surface. They crowded into other words like *gossip* and *hypocrite*. I couldn't handle the idea of having someone see the real me. Having my innermost thoughts and sins exposed like that was terrifying. I went back to sleep that night but wrestled with the uneasy feeling the bad dream had left me with. Peace finally came when I was reminded of the truth that as a follower of Christ, my sins were forgiven, and my sin list was wiped clean. If the doctors could really see my secret self when they went in for surgery, they would see a pure heart- not because of anything I've done- but because of what Christ did for me.

The weekend before surgery, my brother drove up from Florida to pick up five of the kids and take them back to his home where he and Steffanie would keep them until I got home from the hospital. My mom drove up from Fort Lauderdale and my oldest sister, Beth, (the one who was subsidizing my health insurance) flew in from California. Beth would stay for a couple of days and Mom planned to stay with Kelsi and Libby, our two oldest girls, until I got home from the hospital.

The night before surgery, I went to bed with a precious peace that I knew could only come from the Lord. We had to be at the hospital very early the next morning, but before that, I had to take a special sanitizing shower. Unfortunately, I didn't wake up with that same peace that I had been experiencing for weeks. I woke up startled by the realization that it was the day for me to have my chest opened. My body was paralyzed, and my chest felt heavy. I literally couldn't move. I just laid there and wondered what would happen if I just stayed in bed and chose not to go to the hospital. If I didn't show up, then they couldn't do the surgery. But I needed the surgery so I not-so-bravely reminded myself that irrational thoughts wouldn't get me anywhere (although I didn't want to go *anywhere* at that moment).

The week before, one of my sons was playing at the park with a few of his buddies when I overheard them setting up their make-believe fun. They were assigning roles as I heard one of them say, "I wanna be the brave one." And another, "No, *I* want to be the brave one." They went around and around trying to decide who would get to be the brave one that time. The morning of my surgery, I *didn't* want to be the brave one. I had been the brave one so many times before, but on that morning all I wanted to do was kiss courage good-bye and pull the covers over my head.

I still wish that would have been an option, but it wasn't. I had to get up. I had to take that shower. I had to check myself in at the hospital and I had to have open heart surgery. Instead of thinking about tackling all of that at once, I decided to break the morning into bite size chunks. First, I prayed for the courage to get out of bed- and it came. As I sat on the edge of the bed, I prayed for strength to walk to the bathroom. With each step I took towards the bathroom, I then prayed for courage to take the pre-surgery sanitation shower. It came. Not a day's worth of courage, but just enough for that task. Next, I asked the Lord for courage to get dressed and it was there.

When I stood in my closet that morning, praying for strength to get dressed, I decided on an easy outfit, jeans and a t-shirt, so I could quickly get onto the next step before losing my courage. It would be the last time I would comfortably dress myself for several weeks. As I finished getting dressed, my eyes were drawn to an orange sleeve that seemed to have forced its way out from in between the other hanging clothes. The black stripes running vertically down the sleeve immediately identified it as my Boston Marathon jacket. I reached for it and with intentionality and resolve, I slid my left arm into a sleeve and then my right. I then pulled it up over my shoulders and held it around my neck, bringing my fists together in front of my heart. That day, that heart would stop beating.

I decided to wear that jacket to the hospital. I would wear it as a reminder to my family of what I had done. I wore it that day as a way to show the medical personnel at the hospital that I wasn't just a heart patient. I was so much more than just a girl struggling for survival, covered by a thin and nondescript hospital gown.

But the main reason I chose to wear that jacket on that day was because *I* needed the reminder. I needed to be reminded that, although my husband was a huge supporter and encourager to me during my long months of training to qualify for the Boston Marathon, running it was something that I ultimately had to do alone. Yes, Kelsi watched the younger children while I was out there reaching for my goal and a few of the kiddos rode their bikes next to me on some of those miles. Casey often drove the car behind me to light the way and to offer me protection on those crazy-early runs. But even with all that help, no one could step in and do it for me. Supportive they were but substitute they could not. Every step of the hundreds of lonely miles that I covered in order to build the speed and endurance to run just over 8 minutes per mile for 26.2 miles had to be taken by me. And on surgery day, I knew I would have their full support, as usual, but no one could go into the OR as a substitute for me. I had to take every step. And so that jacket, worn that day, was a reminder of that.

By the time I was dressed, the steps towards getting to the hospital were stringing together with fluidity. Getting to the car...

walking into the hospital... putting a smile on my face.... on and on, one step at a time. It all strung together into a peace-filled *early* morning. The Lord gave me the same strength, courage, peace and even humor that he had given all along. It was all there for me. I just had to ask. Yeah, there were times in all of that when I didn't want to be the brave one, but those were the times I had to remind myself that sometimes courage doesn't come all at once.

12

The Heart of Courage

Casey and I drove to the hospital hand-in-hand while my mom and Beth followed in a separate car behind us. Once at the hospital, they sat as I checked in wearing blue jeans and, of course, my Boston jacket. Beth snapped a picture of me at check-in and posted it on Facebook. That began her job of updating friends and family on my progress.

The surgery was a success and I woke up in the cardiac intensive care unit (CICU), surrounded by a circle of close family looking down on me like my kids and I do when we find a turtle on the side of the road. We circle up around it, stare down and wonder what it will do next. I scanned the faces confused about where I was and why they were staring at me like that but in a moment I remembered. I had just had my chest cut open, split apart and my heart stopped so that I could have an artery uprooted and re-implanted. I had spent some time on the Internet learning what I would be hooked up to immediately following surgery so, even under the influence of heavy drugs, I wasn't surprised or bothered by the 16 different lines and tubes that were keeping me alive. My mom and sister gushed over me and told me how good I looked.

Casey later told me that they were lying and that I looked like death. Although he didn't let anybody know it then, he later confided in me telling me that he was terribly bothered by seeing me like that. He was also once again sickened by the familiar smell of cut bone and did all he could to show a strong front.

Over our 19 years of marriage, Casey had seen me through seven births, one miscarriage, a D and C, many medical scans and test, two pre-ops for major surgeries, a heart catheterization, one brain surgery and now a heart surgery. Being my caregiver in so many different capacities only tethered our hearts more tightly together. So instead of it getting easier, seeing me like he saw me that day in CICU was only more difficult. When you share a love that has weathered so much together, you hurt deeply for one another in ways that a young, fresh, infatuation-filled love can't understand. In fact, our love for one another has grown into something so strong and deep that, looking back at how we felt towards one another when we first got married, I often wonder if we even knew what love was then.

It was that kind of love that kept Casey by my hospital bed for the next seven days, caring for me in ways that still overwhelm me. The day after my surgery, I started my period. I had a catheter in, so I couldn't wear underwear. However, the hospital staff was making me get out of bed so pads weren't an option for handling my cycle at that point. I was pretty bothered by the predicament because I didn't want anyone to have to take care of *that* for me. It was humbling and degrading on my end, and I hated putting that task on anyone else, but I certainly couldn't do it. The nurse reassured me that it was part of her job, but I couldn't stand the idea of her having to do it. My husband hesitated for a moment before he stepped in and, in the most selfless act of love I can imagine, he took care of my feminine needs for the duration of my cycle.

With a cocktail of medicines flowing through my veins, I was nauseous for those first few days and didn't want to eat anything. Casey took it upon himself to find any foods that sounded even remotely appetizing to me. If I mentioned that a certain food sounded appealing, he would rush out, a man on a mission, and return beaming with his food offering, only to find that my desire for that food had passed. Undeterred, he encouraged me to eat and was ready to run out again the next time I had the slightest craving for anything.

He watched my body swell, my catheter bag fill, my chest tube drain, and my heart rhythms pulse on a monitor. He learned the ICU lingo and the names of all the nurses. My recovery was his one and only focus. The amazing thing is, I don't think it was a conscious decision on his part to be all in, putting his own needs aside. Loving me with such intensity was just what came out of him naturally. With him by my bedside, we often joked or sometimes just exchanged smiles. He would kiss my forehead and my hand or rub my feet and read me messages from loved ones wishing me well and sending their love. Our love, devotion and commitment grew stronger from those days than they ever could have while lounging next to each other on a tropical beach getaway. Of course, if we could have chosen between the two, we both would have chosen the vacation, but the kind of heart ties we have now could only have come through the valley experiences we we've trudged through together. With someone so loving by my side, taking care of me in the most intimate of ways, it wasn't hard to dig deep to find the courage to give my best towards my recovery each day.

When I was a runner in high school, proudly sporting the Bulldogs' maroon and gold, my coach used to get on me for smiling while I was running. Coach Mac was one of a kind with a voice that could never be forgotten. In his signature raspy yell, he would call out to me (using my maiden name) as I ran by him in a race, "Ansbaugh, if you're smiling then you're not giving it your all!" I'd try to wipe the smile off my face to please the man I highly respected but as soon as I'd pass him by, a new smile would replace the old one. I later learned that runners who smile while pounding the pavement have a lower perceived rate of exertion. I didn't know that I was implementing exercise science when I was smiling on runs, it just felt like the right thing to do as I ran past supporters who were giving their time to cheer me on. After my surgery, I took that same attitude as I stepped through each phase of my recovery. I smiled because it made me feel better and hopefully encouraged others around me.

My days in the hospital were brightened by sweet visits from friends and family and especially by afternoon visits from Mom, Kelsi and Libby. Beth had since returned to California and the girls were spending their days with my mom. She would bring them up in the afternoons when they would tell Casey and I about their adventures together that day. Once again, mom was there when we needed her the most. She had put a week of her life on hold to make sure that Kelsi and Libby's days of uncertainty while their mom was in the hospital were spent making happy memories.

My dad also made the trip up to see me in the hospital. Visiting with him also brightened my little ICU space. We reminisced about the time when I was about twelve-years-old and I brought home a kitten for him for Father's Day. Daddy wasn't especially fond of cats, but I sure was! I knew if the kitten was a gift to him, he couldn't refuse. That cat, whom we named Boots, ended up being the gift that kept on giving as it became the father of generations of cats that filled our yard over the years that followed that infamous Father's Day. Dad laughed as we remembered that story and I tried hard not to laugh because my chest hurt so badly when I did. He also reminded me of the time he came home from work and as he walked toward the back door, he was passed by nearly a half-dozen punk rock cats (all Boots' offspring, no doubt). I had used hair spray and scissors to give all of the cats make overs. Dad said he never knew what to expect from me when he came home from work. I'm sure in all his years as my daddy he never expected to see me dependent on all those wires and tubes. As hard as it must have been to see his little cat-loving, pageant girl all grown up, swollen, and attached to so many tubes and wires, his focus was on making me happy, which was true to his character.

I spent an extra day or two in ICU because of swelling and was finally deemed ready to be moved to a regular cardiac room. But before I could be moved, I had to have two lead lines pulled from my chest. These electrical wires had been inserted through my skin under my left breast and then attached to my heart. When it was time for them to come out, a nurse had me take a deep breath and then with one swift pull, she yanked them off my heart and through my skin. With less lines attached to me and the swelling under control, I should have been making progress and working towards getting discharged. Instead, I fought headaches, lacking energy and motivation. That trio of problems was an unusual combination for me, even for just having heart surgery. The doctors soon discovered that my blood levels were low and strongly suggested that I receive a blood transfusion. I didn't want to have anything to do with that idea. Cut open my chest, fine. Turn off my heart, OK. Even yank wires out of my body like it's nothing. But send someone else's blood pulsing through my veins? No way. I had been a blood donor many times and supported the practice but the thought of being on the receiving end of the procedure really bothered me. If I had had the energy to fight the idea, maybe I would have. But I was weak and making slow progress. The medical staff had been giving me supplements through IV that should have fixed the problem, but they didn't work, leaving the transfusion as my only option. I half-heartedly agreed and within the hour, a nurse was setting up to begin the transfusion. I had the courage to consent to the procedure but that was as far as I was going with the whole courage thing when it came to a transfusion. Instead of facing it head on, I decided to turn my head, close my eyes and take my mind to someplace else until it was over. I didn't want to see the bag of blood, the red IV lines or the needle in my arm.

That dreaded transfusion ended up being a turning point in my recovery. A complete stranger who had chosen to donate the very blood that had once pumped through their own veins- a fact that grossed me out- had become the very surge of help I needed to get well. My energy returned quickly, and I was finally able to make some progress towards getting out of the hospital. The next step in my release was to have a port removed from my neck. I'm sure every heart surgery patient would give differing opinions on this, but for me, having the port removed was the worst part of the whole ordeal. Even now as I write about it, 5 years later, I can still feel the tube coming out of my neck and the nurse putting full pressure on the open wound for 15 minutes before bandaging it up. Once again, I had to occupy my mind with distant thoughts, mantras, breathing and Bible verses to mentally remove myself from the discomfort.

On the day I was to go home, it brought me joy to see Casey sorting discharge papers and helping me get dressed into regular clothes to leave the hospital. Just as Casey was helping me put on my shirt, Dr. Johnson came in to tell us that I wouldn't be going home after all. The hospital staff had been taking chest x-rays of me daily but the image from that that morning had shown fluid buildup around my lungs in my chest cavity. Instead of getting ready to go home, I would have to get ready to go to the radiology department to have an imaging-guided draining procedure performed to get rid of the fluid.

We were surprised by the news because I felt fine and we were so ready to go home. We quickly reminded ourselves that our goal was for me to be well and to have a full recovery. This was just another small step in the big picture of my recovery, so we trusted the Lord to guide it, as he had done with every other step. Once phone calls were made to make arrangements for our children's care, we settled back into our hospital room, waiting for someone to come take me to radiology.

To have the fluid removed, I was taken to a stale room where a large needle was inserted into my back to drain out the fluid. Yet again, the Lord gave me the courage and mental strength to remove myself from overthinking what was being done to me. When I saw the large amount of yellow fluid that had been extracted from my chest cavity, I couldn't believe the nasty stuff had come out of my body! I asked the technician to save the container to show to Casey, knowing he would be impressed. He wasn't. Instead he was grossed out and refused to look. I should have known better! We would be able to go home in a couple more days, once the doctor was confident that the fluid they had removed wasn't being replaced by my body.

I was so ready to go home, but after being in the hospital for a week, I found it a little sad to leave the staff who had given so much of themselves to keep me alive. They had seen me through several setbacks, staying committed to helping me move forward. I was particularly amazed by the young people entering the field of nursing, knowing that with all the disgusting parts of their job that they had to do on a daily basis, they had to be in it for more than the money. Each one seemed to bring their heart into their work to provide much more than just physical care for my body. Seeing this type of generosity in action gave me a renewed hope in our younger generations.

On our way home from the hospital, we stopped at a pharmacy to pick up my prescriptions. Casey went in to get the medications while I sat in the car, holding onto the stuffed "Heart Surgery Bear" the hospital had given me. Casey's phone rang. It was "Uncle Bro," Isaiah's uncle. Though we had been praying for Isaiah since he left our house the previous summer, we hadn't heard from him in ten months. The conversation was choppy, but I soon realized that Uncle Bro was asking me if we were interested in becoming Isaiah's Forever Family. Tears welled up in my eyes and my heart started skipping beats- literally- which wasn't good. I took a few deep breaths to gain control of my emotions and asked, "You haven't heard what we've just gone through, have you?" He hadn't. "Well, I just had open heart surgery and am on my way home from the hospital. We *do* want Isaiah," I told him with every bit of conviction I had in me, "but we need a little time," I went on. "Right now, I can't even take care of the children we have, but if you guys can wait a few weeks, we can meet up with you and talk." He agreed and we hung up.

When Casey got back to the car, I gave him the exciting news. Months before, we had agreed to wait until we "were on the other side of the heart situation" before we pursued Isaiah and there we were, driving home from the hospital when we got the call, just "on the other side". I think we had figured we would be a little more "on the other side" before we pursued him though! It was also amazing to me that in the months since we had last seen Isaiah, I had those dreams about him. It wasn't until that moment in the car, after hanging up on the phone with Uncle Bro that I put together that in all of the dreams, they had brought Isaiah to us and we didn't even have to pursue. That's exactly what happened that day in the pharmacy parking lot when I got the phone call. They were giving him to us and, though our hearts were aching to have him, we didn't have to go after him. Of course, we would have gone to the ends of the earth for him, but the way it all fit together confirmed for us that we were walking in God's will.

I didn't want to tell Casey how the emotions I had felt while on the phone with Uncle Bro had affected my heart. He was so protective of me so I knew it would bother him. I wanted all the feels that came with finding out that there was a huge possibility that Isaiah would be our son. I wanted to let my mind picture what it would be like to tell the kids and the rest of our family. Everything in me wanted to imagine the reunion between Isaiah and the rest of our children. I wanted to wonder what the adoption process would look like, but I had to stuff all of that in order to let my heart heal. Losing our sweet little baby number eight and then the Lord giving us Isaiah instead also brought on a snowball of feelings that I just physically couldn't let myself tap into yet.

Through all of it, I was learning that being courageous isn't always about having the strength to walk headlong into a situation. Yes, sometimes courage is letting myself feel the full force of emotions and letting them wholly run their course until healing comes. But, at other times, courage is having the strength to put my mind on other things so that my body can handle the hurt or discomfort it was being put through. And as I learned that day on the way home from the hospital, sometimes courage requires delaying emotions so other parts can heal first. This may have been the toughest form of courage I had encountered yet.

Casey and I pulled up to our home at Camp Grace to find my mom, Kelsi, and Libby waiting on the front porch for us. They had decorated the porch with signs and a banner to give me a royal welcome. It felt so good to be home.

The day after I got home from the hospital was Patriot's Day- the Monday that the Boston Marathon is run on every year. I was registered for that race and had started to train for it before all of my heart problems rose to the surface. Of course, I wouldn't be running that year. But on race day, I sat in my pajamas in my recliner with a chest full of staples and wondered if I would ever run again. My body felt so frail and tattered. I had endured so much that in that moment it was hard to imagine my weak legs cruising down roads and crossing finish lines ever again. As I was lost in thought, aware of the race being run in Boston while I sat feebly in my chair 7 days post-op, a package was delivered to our front door. Casey brought the box and opened it for me. My eyes got misty as he pulled a brand-new pair of running shoes from the box along with a note from Bernard, the guy I had run the Boston Marathon with the year before. Bernard had been messaging with Casey through Facebook to find out our address and my shoe size. Together they worked out the details to make sure that the shoes would arrive during the running of the 2014 Boston Marathon as a message to me that Bernard believed I would indeed run again. I chose to agree with him and focused on getting well so I could lace up those new shoes!

Once all of the kids were back home with us, Amy drove up from Florida to spend her days at our house and to help keep things running smoothly while I recovered. She didn't quit her job for this surgery like she did when I had brain surgery. This time she brought her laptop and worked on keeping her new screen printing business afloat from afar. It meant so much to me that she was there again to keep me company. She was also committed to preparing healthy meals for me and to keep charge of the kids. A lot had changed since my brain surgery- we lived in a different state, the kids were all 10 years older (and so were we), we had two more children, Amy was running a successful business with her partner, Dani, and she had survived stage 3 cancer- but our heart connection remained.

When it came to my recovery, I followed the doctor's orders carefully. After having Josie and then going out and running hard before my body was ready, I had learned that healing once the first time and avoiding complications was the way to go. It took more patience right out of the gate, but it ensured that I would heal completely in the long run. I made sure I drank the recommended amount of water each day. As instructed, I didn't lift anything heavier than the water bottle the nurses sent home with me. I also weighed myself regularly to check for fluid retention, took daily naps and slowly built up a modest walking routine.

The first time I set out for a walk, Casey met me on the front porch with the shoes that Bernard had sent me. While the horses grazed peacefully in a field nearby, Casey put the shoes on me and laced them up. We walked hand-in-hand down the front steps and walked about a quarter of a mile, which took nearly 30 minutes. I was slow and fragile, but I was outside in the fresh air with the love of my life and I was wearing running shoes!

13

Courage Lost

I was doing great in my open heart surgery recovery. I was actually surprised with how smoothly everything was going. Following Dr. Johnson's orders, I was taking it easy, mixing short periods of light activity followed by rest. My range of motion was increasing while my pain level was decreasing. Each day, I felt stronger than the day before.

Thirteen days after my open heart surgery, the camp was hosting a church group for the weekend while my oldest son, Gunner, was being trained on the camp's high ropes course. It seemed that Gunner had spent more of his life off the ground than on it, starting his climbing at 11 months old when he scaled to the top of our dining room table. I decided to make the quarter mile walk to watch him train, knowing that all the years of seeing him defy gravity in heart-stopping ways would finally make sense.

It took me 30 minutes to make the walk and I looked like a 90-year-old, complete with shuffling feet and slouched shoulders, but I made that walk. When I got to my destination, I felt accomplished, but I also took comfort in knowing that I hadn't done too much. I walked, like the doctor told me to do. I took it slow and didn't push myself. Casey had arranged for me to have a chair so I could rest at the high ropes course, which was situated at the edge of a Georgian pine forest. I sat in the shade, watching my adept son in his element. As the sun made its way up in the sky, camp visitors and staff came and went and so did the morning. I knew that the quarter mile walk back to our on-site home, which was mostly uphill, would be asking too much of my healing body so I hitched a slow and easy golf cart ride back home. I had lunch and took my self-prescribed daily nap in an automatic recliner that we had borrowed from a friend.

A couple of hours after I woke up, I decided to join my family for dinner with the visiting retreat group in the camp cafeteria. Six months before, I was taken from that same cafeteria with severe chest pain. Months later, I was on the other side of heart surgery and back to the cafe for the first time since the surgery. It was a tenth of a mile walk, which I took slowly, even though I felt fine. But as I visited with an acquaintance over one of my favorite camp-made meals, I began to feel uncomfortably full, even though I'd only eaten a few bites. I smiled through the conversation but grew more and more uncomfortable as the minutes wore on. I walked home as my thoughts were torn between feeling content in the day's accomplishments and wondering why my stomach all of a sudden felt so full and troublesome.

In keeping with our new, but temporary, system Casey got the kids to bed and then came to get me settled in the non-automated recliner in the family room. This was my bed until I could once again lay flat and enjoy going to bed next to my partner. This was probably the worst part of the recovery for me-sleeping in the recliner and away from my man. I knew he didn't like it either. He saw to my needs, which were many, and I wondered how often he wanted to smother me with a pillow after having to adjust it for me a dozen times. It turned out that getting comfortable isn't easy after having your chest cracked open. Casey supplied me with what was my usual: water, a blanket, the TV remote and our home phone (so we wouldn't repeat the night that I needed to get up in the night but couldn't yell out loud enough to wake him). But that night I also asked for a puke bucket because I just didn't feel well. All I could tell him was that I felt so full. Just. So. Full. But I didn't even eat much for dinner. I was baffled. He kissed my forehead, prayed for me and then headed to bed. I decided to post an update on Facebook about my successful day and to share how well I was doing. After typing a few words, I deleted the update, realizing the irony in that, yes, I was making progress, but at that moment, I felt sicker than I had in a very long time. I decided to turn on the TV to help get my mind off my angst but after realizing the only thing playing on our limited stations was a television evangelist selling holy water, I actually felt worse.

I finally drifted off to sleep but woke up aware of my worsening condition several times in the night. I picked up the phone to call Casey and then put it down realizing that my only complaint was the feeling of being full. There was nothing I could do about it and I think I was most concerned about what pain I would experience if I had to throw up with a sternum that had been cut apart less than two weeks before. I fell asleep again waking up to the sun streaming in the windows of an unusually quiet house.

Casey and the kids were at the cafe for breakfast so there appeared to be no one home to help me out of the recliner. I managed somehow to get up and head to the bathroom. I felt terribly sick to my stomach and nearly passed out when I finally made it to the bathroom. It was all I could do to make it back to the living room, where I practically collapsed on the couch. I started to rack my brain to figure out what was wrong with me. I was doing so well and making progress. My heart felt fine and I hadn't over exerted myself.

Surprisingly, as I was lost in thought, my sweet Kelsi May stepped into the room. It turned out she'd been home all along. She saw that I wasn't feeling well and was so thoughtful to ask what she could do to help me. I wasn't sure. I felt that I needed my pain medication but didn't want to take it on an empty stomach. I couldn't eat, however, because my stomach was so upset. I decided I needed to get up and walk to see if I could get the full feeling gone, which I had begun to think was gas. She helped me stand up, but I was back on the couch in seconds because I was so light-headed.

We decided to call Casey but thankfully he walked in the house at the moment Kelsi was reaching for the phone. As I explained my symptoms, which added up to feeling full, nauseated, and faint, we just didn't know what to do or what was wrong. Casey wanted to call the doctor, but I didn't want to bother Dr. Johnson on a Sunday. We finally agreed to call our friend Dottie, who was a cardiac nurse. After hearing my symptoms, she advised me to call the doctor right away, go straight to the ER, or call an ambulance. I told her there was no way I was going to call an ambulance but that I would put a call into the doctor. Dottie told me that she thought my issue had something to do with too much fluid, so I called for a scale before calling the doctor. I had been weighing myself at the same time every day per discharge orders to watch for extra fluid retention.

Casey brought out the scale and set it on the floor near the couch. It took all the strength I had to walk a few steps to the scale and get back to the couch. I had gained several pounds in 24 hours. This was not good. In just the few steps it took to get back to the couch and within minutes of hanging up with Dottie, things started happening to me that I struggle to find the words to explain. In a single moment, I took a horrific turn for the worse that forced me into a living nightmare. I began to lose consciousness. As that happened, I didn't merely pass out, but I felt as if a powerful and fearsome force was pulling me from life to death. My body convulsed. I vomited while Casey stood by pleading for me to come back. I came to just in time to see my terrified daughter begin to get hysterical. It must have looked as bad as it felt. I'd passed out several times in my life but that losing of consciousness was like nothing I'd ever experienced.

Casey called the ambulance, left a message for the doctor and called my sister, who was already on her way over to help for the day. Before long, our house was a flurry of activity. Kelsi was packing a hospital bag for us but was also terrified and sobbing. The camp founder's wife, Susie, had slipped in and was by my side praying quietly over me. Our camp director, Lucas, who was EMT trained, had come in to check on my vitals and to just be there with Casey until we were on the ambulance. Others were trying to make sure they were with our other kids, keeping them in an area of Camp where they wouldn't see the ambulance when it came in. Several friends were on the porch praying.

Casey was fanning me with a small paperback book while a couple of people kept rotating out cool wash clothes for my forehead. All my strength had left and what little I had was spent on staying conscious. Silently, I was praying, reciting scripture in my head, focusing on objects, memories… basically anything I could do to keep controlled, relaxed and "alert." I knew that if I lost control of my emotions, it would only be worse for me.

I was also occasionally pleading with Casey, whether in a few words or in look, for him not to let me slip out of it again. I truly felt that I wouldn't come back. I wasn't afraid of death. As a follower in Christ, I had a complete peace about the afterlife, but the horrific way in which I was losing consciousness made me fear the actual process of dying.

Inside, I was also hoping for the ambulance to come soon. We knew we could have made it to the hospital faster than the ambulance could get to us out at that rural camp, but we knew I couldn't even get *to* the car. We also knew that being taken right into the ER from the ambulance would be smoother as the hospital staff would be forewarned of, and therefor prepared for, my arrival. I turned my focus to seeing the ambulance pull up and used those thoughts to help me pull through. Two people at Camp Grace were given the job of guiding the ambulance drivers past other camp buildings to our house.

It ended up taking 35 minutes for the ambulance to arrive. Our local ambulance company had only two vehicles in service, one which was already out on a call. The other had to come from near the hospital, which was in Macon, almost forty minutes away. Once at our house, the EMTs did a quick assessment and then loaded me on a gurney. Casey continued to faithfully fan me to help keep me comfortable as possible. As we were on our way out of the house, I noticed that the book he was using to fan me belonged to a set of reading books that we had used to teach all of our children to read. Even in my near-death state, the homeschool mom in me kicked in and I weakly asked him to switch the book out for one that didn't belong to the set. I was sure that if that book made it out of our house, it would never find its way back. He obliged, but only because I was in such critical condition. Had I been feeling a little better, he may have decided to whack me over the head with that tiny paperback book for being so particular in such a dire time!

As our responders became aware of the state of my vital signs on the way to the hospital, they remained clueless as to the cause of my symptoms. They chose to drive the 40 miles to the hospital with no lights or sirens and at regular speed, stopping at every stop sign and light. One of the men told me reassuringly that they chose to drive at that speed so that they wouldn't make me concerned or anxious. After waiting over a half of an hour for the ambulance to arrive, we found comfort in knowing we would get there quickly in an emergency vehicle. Knowing that the driver was making the trip as slow as possible actually made us feel unsettled and confused. My fight between consciousness and that dark abyss I experienced had calmed down a bit on the ride to the hospital and I felt a bit more comfortable than I had in the moments leading up to the ambulance's arrival. Nevertheless, I still spent the entire ride thinking that I would feel so much better when my care was out of the hands of the EMTs and in the care of the hospital staff. The technician attending to me spent the entire ride trying to figure out why he couldn't get a pulse- ox reading on me. He tried every oximeter and method he could think of to get a reading on me but never connected the lack of a reading to the possibility that I was having a serious complication related to my heart surgery.

When we got to the hospital, Casey heard the man in the back of the ambulance ask the driver to back out of sight of the hospital doors because he had forgotten to call ahead to let the ER staff know we were coming. The guys didn't want to look inept, so they backed up the vehicle and called in before they would become visible to the folks in the ER. Between that and some of the questions they asked like, "Do you have a history of chest pain?" all while I had 35 staples and a seven-inch incision down the center of my chest, left me feeling very much like we were in an episode of Gomer Pyle.

Unfortunately, my care didn't improve when I was taken in to the critical care unit of the ER. Despite the fact that I felt as if I were barely hanging onto life, no one was rushing or had any sense of urgency about them. There were several times that Casey and I were the only ones left in the room. My eyes would plead for him to do something to help speed things up, but I also didn't want him to leave my side because he was fanning me, bringing me the only comfort I had from head to toe.

One of the big hold ups in the ER (as it was in the ambulance) was that no one could get my pulse ox. Instead of realizing that my heart was failing, and my pressures were too weak to detect, the nurses wasted time trying different equipment, cords and even getting oximeters from the pediatric area. No one seemed to connect my symptoms with my very recent heart surgery. I was quickly dying. Even the MD on call came in, introduced himself and told me they would do a few tests throughout the day to see if I was having a gallbladder attack because of my stomach pain and nausea. It was as if the fact that I had had heart surgery so recently that I still had the staples in my chest was irrelevant to him. I weakly reminded the doctor that I wasn't experiencing stomach pain per say but that I was feeling a sensation of fullness and pain in my upper abdomen and was nauseated and experiencing symptoms of shock. As he explained to me what he was going to give me for symptoms, making no effort to find a cause, I wanted so desperately to convey to him that I needed something quickly and couldn't hold on much longer.

The ER doctor finally decided to call Dr. Johnson, my surgeon, and Dr. Johnson immediately asked him what my heart looked like. The ER doctor hadn't even looked at my heart! When he hung up with the surgeon, he immediately brought an ultrasound machine to my bedside to do an echocardiogram. After less than 10 seconds of viewing my heart on the screen, he dropped the wand onto my chest and rushed out to call Dr. Johnson back.

In the meantime, my hands had turned a purplish grey and were causing me discomfort. Casey looked and wore the stunned look on his face as he told me, "They're purple." My feet were also numb, tingling and cold, so I asked him to check them, too. He confirmed that they were also purple. Before long, I felt a very cold sensation taking over. My heart was shutting down and was ceasing to deliver blood to my extremities. I was faintly telling Casey that I was barely holding on as he tirelessly fanned me in an effort to keep me conscious. I had never felt so desperate and sick in my life. I finally mouthed to Casey, "I'm dying." I lost consciousness only to be pulled back vomiting and convulsing. This happened again and again. I should have been thankful to wake up each time. I would love to say that I fought hard every moment. But I was in such extreme physical distress that I no longer cared if I woke up again or not. I just wanted to be disconnected from my physical body. If that meant being medically "put out", then great, but I was also at the point that if only death would save me from the horror, then I was OK with that, too.

When the heart surgeon arrived, he began to put a fire under everyone. He brought in an ultrasound tech and I remember him commenting out loud to her that there was more fluid than there was heart and that the entire right side of my heart was compressed from the fluid. At some point he leaned in to me, cupped my face in his skilled hands and asked me to open my eyes. I obeyed, using all of my focus to look at him. "You have too much fluid around your heart. I'm going to create a window into the sac around the heart and drain the fluid, OK?" That man who had snapped at me the first time I met him, leaving me feeling uncomfortable in his care was about to save my life, for a second time, and he did it with the perfect balance of professionalism and compassion. From the time I had arrived at the emergency room, everything had felt so disorganized and scattered but, in that moment, with Dr. Joe Johnson in charge, things felt peaceful and under control.

Once Dr. Johnson gave orders for getting everything in place for surgery, he returned to my side to monitor my blood pressure. The last time Casey remembered seeing my blood pressure reading, it was 60/30 and with that, our very competent surgeon, who I'd grown to love and respect, grabbed my gurney and took my life into his own hands. He personally rolled me to the operating room. As he wheeled me, he made arrangements for Casey to be taken to a waiting area. He was there to save me, but he was also concerned for Casey and wanted to be sure that he knew where he was so that he would be able to find him after surgery. I appreciated that.

I was rolled into the OR and placed on a hard, flat, narrow table, which only caused me more discomfort. I winced in pain. My incision was prepped three times with vigorous scrubbing and swabbing which elicited more moans from me. At the same time, someone put a mask on me over the supplemental oxygen that I was already receiving. The mask had rubber edges around it and in my disoriented state, it felt like it was cutting off my air supply instead of helping me in anyway. My frail body was laid out bare on a flat operating table with medical personnel swarming about me. My sore chest was being scrubbed with disinfecting chemicals, and I felt like I couldn't breathe. As the mask was being pressed tighter to my face, I managed to turn my head to the side and get a gasp of air. In all the hurry of putting together an operating room staff for me to have emergency surgery and getting my chest ready for surgery, I grew concerned that the staff would forget to actually put me to sleep. I couldn't bear the thought of being awake while they cut into my chest. I struggled to move the mask over just a bit and drew in another breath and then gasped out loud, "I'm still awake, I'm still awake!"

Looking back, I find it funny that I was so concerned about my modesty in that first appointment with Dr. Johnson. I was insistent that I not be exposed even though I would be asleep and wouldn't know the difference. Two weeks after the initial surgery, I was back on the operating table, fully awake and aware that my chest was completely bare, but it was the last thing on my mind. After I felt a few bursts of what felt like acid in my IV, my greatest desire was granted, and I was finally put out. While I slept, the surgeon removed 8-9 staples from my chest and re-opened the bottom 1.5 inches of my existing incision. He created a pericardial window and drained 500 cc of fluid from the sac around my heart. Normal fluid levels around the heart are only 20-50 cc.

Casey told me later on that he had been alone in the waiting room and was at his end emotionally. That morning was like a hurricane and when they wheeled me into surgery, I was so unstable that he just couldn't think straight. He was just to his breaking point when my sister, Amy, also shell-shocked, came in. They both hugged and cried until the emotional pressure had been released. Before long, friends filled the room, staying by Casey's side until I came safely out of surgery. Casey's dad from North Carolina, and my brother from Florida, had both heard about the emergency and jumped into their cars, driving hours to be with us. I found out later that heaven was also filling up with prayers on my behalf from people all over who heard of the urgent prayer request.

I was partially awake in the recovery room but would never allow myself to open my eyes. I only wanted to be asleep or at least have everyone think I was asleep so no one would bother me.

I didn't want to talk, to move or to be poked or prodded. I just wanted to lie there and not feel a thing. There was another patient in recovery who was having a difficult time with all of the tubes so she was demanding all of the nurses' attention. I remember feeling relieved that they were focused on her and hoped that they wouldn't notice me.

I had endured too much. Too much pain. Too much shock. Too much horror. I just needed to be left alone to drift in and out of sleep and to begin to decompress from the ordeal. All at one time, there were so many emotions to sort through and yet they were partially clouded by the lingering meds that had been forced through my veins to get me to sleep quickly. There was the emotional equivalent of catching my breath from the whirlwind I had just experienced. There was the disappointment that I was worse off than I had been when I woke up in ICU from OHS just 13 days before. I also struggled with guilt as I tried to figure out if something I had done had caused this to happen to me. With the image of Casey's distressed look as I was wheeled away, my mind also wondered how he was doing and if he knew I was OK. Of course, I was also brimming over with thankfulness that I had made it through the horrific ordeal. But even the thankfulness was somewhat drowned out by the overwhelming flood of imagery that replayed the day's tragic scenes over and over in my head. The vomiting, the convulsing, the loss of consciousness. Kelsi's uncontrollable crying as she watched helplessly. The unbearable physical weight of the shock my body had suffered through. The ambulance ride. The doctor who acted like we had all day to figure things out and the nurses flitting from room to room trying to get the right equipment, leaving Casey and I alone to face death. My hands and feet turning grey. Feeling the life being sucked out of me. Hearing my surgeon say that the right side of my heart was completely compressed. It was too much to bear. I was, in every sense of the word, traumatized. I couldn't speak, I didn't want to speak. I didn't want to be awake. And I didn't want to be noticed. I just wanted to be left alone.

"God won't give us more than we can handle," is one of my least favorite sayings and I'm living proof that he does indeed give us more than we can bear. I knew what I suffered through, just that one day, that one trial, was beyond anything I could have handled on my own. What I've come to learn is that God does give us more than we can handle so we learn to lean into him for the courage needed for each weary step we take on the uncertain path before us.

We learned later that I had experienced a complication from my surgery called cardiac tamponade. We discovered that there is a widely used and taught assessment for the condition that our emergency responders should have been aware of. I had all of the markers they should have been looking for and that even my heart tones would have been noticeably muffled if *just one* medical caregiver would have put a stethoscope on my chest to listen to my heart.

The overall mortality risk with cardiac tamponade depends on the speed of diagnosis and the treatment provided. Untreated, the condition is rapidly and universally fatal. Despite the slow ride to the hospital with EMTs who seemed more concerned about their reputations than they did about getting me immediately to the life-saving care I needed, my life was spared. In spite of the ER staffs' lack of urgency and knowledge, and their incompetence regarding my care, the Lord had sustained me. And though I even got to the point that I no longer wanted to fight for life, my Heavenly Father was in control. Just like I was reminded from Psalm 121 the week before my surgery, my help came from the Lord. Later, when I was able to thank the surgeon at my bedside for what he did for me, he humbly responded with a heavenward gesture and said, "Don't thank me, thank Him."

Eventually, I was wheeled to a room in the same cardiovascular step-down unit that I had spent several days in after my initial surgery. After having done so well after my first surgery I would have *never* guessed that I would end up back in the hospital! I awoke to my sweet husband, who was always by my side, looking extremely relieved. My sister, pastor and other dear friends from church were there, too. I immediately had tears in my eyes because tears were all that would come when I thought of what I had just endured. That whole morning seemed never-ending and only got worse with each passing moment. I had fought to be strong and controlled when it mattered but when the battle for my life was finally over, I had so much pent up emotion that I wanted to release through a flood of tears. I immediately realized that I couldn't allow myself to let the tears fall though because of the pain I was in. The convulsing and vomiting seemed to undo the healing that had taken place over the previous two weeks. While the surgery provided instant relief from the fluid buildup around my heart, it left a fresh wound. I also soon discovered that I had a decent sized drainage tube inserted into my chest that was draining the tremendous amounts of fluid that was still building up around my heart. There was no allowance for the sobbing I wanted to release. I had to be still and controlled for my own good. Once again, I had to find the courage to hold my emotions together until my physical body had gone through some healing. I had to trust that the emotional healing would have to come later.

My brother's humor-filled visits during that hospital certainly helped start the healing. On my first walk down the hospital hall, he lined up next to me saying that he wished we had race numbers pinned to our clothing (mine a hospital gown, of course). He crouched into a starting line racing position and declared that for the first time in several years, he was sure to beat me. I looked at him sideways and smiled a half smile, my broken body hunched over with tubes attached in several places. Even there, after just making it over the biggest hurdle in my life, Chad was lined up next to me ready to use our love for friendly competition to keep me smiling.

It reminded me of a time, over a decade earlier, when we were side by side in an actual competition. Chad had gotten into doing sprint triathlons so, of course, I had to do one with him. On the morning of the triathlon, Chad and I showed up to see over 1,000 racing bikes racked in rows, waiting to be put to the test. Chad surveyed all the expensive bikes and then looked at mine. Shaking his head in dismay he said, "Out of all the bikes here, you have the absolute worst one." He was right. The bike I brought was a Sunday cruiser that didn't even have gears. I had two young children at home (Kelsi was two, Gunner was one, and I was pregnant with Libby, but I didn't know it yet) so I hadn't spent much time or money on preparing for the race. The only step I took to get equipment ready was to take the basket off the handle bars and the baby seat off the back the night before the tri. I shrugged my shoulders at him and went to set up my transition area.

My lack of preparation was noticeable immediately. During the quarter mile swim leg of the race, a race volunteer in a canoe rowed over, offering me help. My custom swim "stroke" apparently made me look like I was drowning. In my defense I did attempt a training swim on the lake we lived on at the time: Alligator Lake. One day, I swam from the shore out to the end of our dock and back, and the next... I saw a large alligator hanging out in the exact spot where I had turned around the day before. That was my first and last training swim, obviously. So, I wasn't surprised to be in dead last place when I got out of that water on race day.

The first few miles of the hilly 12-mile bike ride were lonely. That's what last place feels like. At around the third mile, I saw a lone bike rider ahead of me. As I began to gain on him, I noticed that while he had two legs, he was only pedaling with one of them. I began to gain on him, feeling guilty that the only person I would pass in the entire race was competing with only one functioning leg! Before long, I was close enough to notice that he was holding one of his pedals in his hand and then it hit me that the guy wasn't handicapped- his pedal broke! He didn't train on one leg, he was thrust into the feat less than a quarter of the way into the bike portion of the race. I immediately thought *My brother would do that. If his bike was broken, he wouldn't give up either. He would press on, no matter how hard it got.*

I glanced from the pedal in his hand to the man's face as I pulled up beside the courageous rider only to discover that it *was* my big brother. "Chad?" I exclaimed and questioned all at once. He looked over at me, tears rolling down his strained face. He was working so hard out there by himself to get through a race that looked completely different from the one he had envisioned. I felt so bad for him and began to verbally gush over him only the way a younger sister can do when she sees her big brother hurting so badly. When I ran out of things to say, I just rode next to him saying "I'm so sorry" over and over in the annoying way also only a little sister can do. Having me on my cruiser, riding next to him, staring and apologizing non-stop only made his situation worse. "Please just pass me and go on," he instructed. I couldn't imagine leaving him out there by himself and he couldn't imagine riding the next nine miles with his little sis on repeat. I obeyed because the little sister does what the big brother tells her to do. But it hurt to leave him.

Casey, Steff, and I watched Chad finish the final stretch of the 3.1 mile run that finished off his slowest triathlon to date. It was tough to see him wince in pain with each step as he neared the finish line, broken bike pedal still in hand. After getting his finisher's medal, he limped over to a nearby playground slide and sat with his elbows on his knees, head hung low. There's a picture of that moment taped in one of Steffanie's photo albums and forever etched in my mind. It's a picture of victory and defeat all at once. Kind of like how I looked shuffling next to him that day in the hospital. Defeated by an unexpected brush with death but walking, however slowly, in victory. I was sure that Chad learned more about himself during that disappointing finish than he could have ever learned from setting a personal record. That's the way failure teaches us. (Side note: his failure also taught us that I wasn't actually the one with the worst bike that day!)

I was in the hospital for several days with Casey by my side as we watched more and more fluid from around my heart drain from a chest tube that led to a collection bag hanging my bed. Our emotions moved from gratitude that my life had been spared to shock and disbelief that we were back in the hospital again. The cardiac tamponade came on so quickly that we were completely blindsided by the ordeal. The shock to my body caused my cycle to start up again as a protective measure. So once again, Casey's devotion to me propelled him to care for me in ways neither of us would have ever imagined.

A bit of comic relief came during that tragic time when Casey dug through the hospital bag Kelsi had packed for us. To this day, several years later, Kelsi still describes the day I went into shock from cardiac tamponade as the worst day of her life. In her panic, she randomly grabbed items for us, stuffed them in a bag and handed them off to her daddy as he climbed into the ambulance. A couple days after the emergency surgery, I was finally ready to put undergarments on under my hospital gown. As Casey searched our bag, he found that in her haste, Kelsi had unknowingly only packed a sexy little pair of underwear for me. As much as it hurt my chest to laugh, I had a hard time not giggling when Casey pulled them from the bag. I couldn't even imagine putting those things on my swollen and exhausted body! The smiles Casey and I shared over that mix-up felt so good after the trauma we had both just experienced. Laughter really is the best medicine.

14

Courage for the Unexpected

As I stepped towards the starting line, I somehow felt strong and frail at the same time. My body was thin and weak looking, my chest scarred and sore. But my mind was ready and my heart was on the mend. Though I'd walked up to countless starting lines and normally felt at home in those pre-race moments, on this day, I felt starkly out of place.

Just weeks before, my very existence was dependent solely upon the machines to which I was hooked. At the starting line, my mind replayed the difficulties I had just scuffling a few feet from my hospital bed to my recliner. As I looked around at the other runners looking so athletic and capable, the scene came to mind of me weakly standing at the sink in my hospital room, trying to wash my hands. It was painful just to press my palms together lightly and rub the soap between my hands. But seven weeks after open heart surgery and only five weeks after my near-death experience with cardiac tamponade, I was getting ready to run a local 5K.

The shock my body experienced from the fluid buildup around my heart and the ensuing emergency surgery caused me to go back to square one in my recovery, leading to accept that my recovery would be long and difficult. And it was difficult, but only for about the first week. After that, my healing seemed to progress exponentially. Most mornings I would wake up in disbelief over how much better I felt that day than the day before. I felt like each night's recovery was equal to what I would have expected it might have taken a week to achieve. I began my short, time consuming walks as soon as I felt able. With the doctor's approval and encouragement, it wasn't long before I was adding in a few steps of light jogging just to see how it felt. Over time, the jogging was making up more of my "walks" than the walking was.

One day, I went out for a half mile walk/jog with Casey and as we jogged back towards our house, we passed the camp cafeteria. A group of camp counselors who knew what a feat it was for me to be running by, was standing in front of the cafeteria, cheering me on! My heart warmed from their encouragement and I finished the run with a huge smile on my face. I was running again. Bernard had predicted it with his delivery of running shoes on the day of the Boston Marathon but no one, myself included, could have guessed that I would I would be back to the sport I loved so soon.

I thought back to the blog I had read about the high school student who had the same congenital defect I had and also went through open heart surgery to fix the problem. I remembered feeling inspired by her return to soccer just six weeks after her surgery and setting my mind on having the same type of success. It took seven weeks for me to line up for the 5K but given that I was more than twice her age and that I endured such a devastating setback two weeks into my recovery, I felt like I had made my goal. I couldn't take any credit for the astonishing progress I had made though. I was just as shocked as everyone around me at how quickly I was healing. Only the Lord could take credit for the healing and for the courage he gave me to get out and try, one baby step at a time, to run again.

When the gun went off at the start of that first post-op 5k, I was immediately passed by a throng of runners. I had learned my lesson from being swept up by the competitive excitement years before when I foolishly ran that 5k just days after having Josie. I knew I felt well enough to cover the distance but also understood that there was still so much healing going on underneath that I wasn't about to risk a setback just to prove myself on the race course. I was out there to take in the joy of running (or walking if I felt it was necessary) on a course that embraces runners at all levels of ability. In fact, one of the things I love most about road races was that they welcome people from all walks of life and all fitness levels. Only at a road race could a first-time runner and a professional athlete participate in the same athletic event. I'd been at the front of some smaller races and that day I was closer to the back, but either way, I was thankful to be part of it.

The running community did not disappoint me that day. Aside from Casey and my kids who came to cheer me on, I didn't know anyone at the race. Yet people along the course cheered for me as if they knew every step of the journey I had been on. They had no idea that just weeks before, I was being pulled between life and death and that that run was in a small way, my comeback. Their spirited support helped me to soar that day.

As I jogged along the race course, I came upon a charming home that was surrounded by a sweet little white picket fence. The landscaping was remarkable, and the exterior decor was inviting. I was appreciating the aesthetics of the property when I noticed a sign in the front yard that said, "Mosquito-Free Zone." Everything about the house looked so perfect and unmarred- a fairy tale existence so well erected that not even mosquitos could spoil the dream. The picture was so contrary to what my life story had become that as I shuffled past, I started to chuckle. As humans, our natural tendency is to build a life of happiness and prosperity, free of pain, troubles and even inconveniences, like mosquitos. Our lives could basically be described as the expenditure of a tremendous amount of energy to avoid any form of struggle.

I thought back to the years that I spent trying to maintain the perfect little life. Yet with all my striving, the difficulty still came. I couldn't keep the house looking perfect, the flowers from wilting and those annoying mosquitos out. All of the difficulty I had faced was out of my control. I was born with two major congenital defects, was at the Boston bombing, had an unborn child die in my womb. Another sweet child taken from my arms and then unexpectedly brought back ten long months later. Even my day-to-day life of homeschooling and raising eight children was nowhere near the perfect picture I had imagined it would be. A good marriage took a ton of work and often needed repair, too.

Looking into the windows of that house on the race course I realized, that while everything looked perfect on the outside and it appeared that the owners were winning at their effort to live that elusive dream life, I had no idea what went on behind that glass. I would have bet though, that no matter how hard they tried to keep out the pests, real life was happening to them too. Families fought. Loved ones got sick. Marriages struggled. There was no spray that could keep those issues away. We all needed courage for the unexpected, yet inevitable, difficulties that life throws our way. I had learned concretely that courage was ours for the taking, given to us by a loving Heavenly Father, who gives us just the amount we need for what faces us at the moment. That truth was enough for me to shake free from the dream of the perfect life and run on towards a different, more eternal goal.

With a huge smile on my face, I finished the 5K, running every step of the way. Casey and the kids cheered me on as I crossed the finish line and we all shared hugs and tears. I was ready to move forward with my life- slowly of course- and put that health crisis behind me. I felt as though I had a new heart and couldn't wait to see, in time, what it could do.

I was sorely disappointed when, a few months after surgery, some of my symptoms returned. My heart began palpitating again when I exerted myself and I was once again experiencing chest pain. I was in disbelief. I had been through so much and had come so far but seemed to find myself back to square one. I told Dr. Kingman about my symptoms and after confirming through tests that the work done on my heart during surgery was intact, she referred me to another doctor in her practice who specialized with the electrical issues of the heart. After more tests, that doctor concluded that I had developed scar tissue at the sight of reimplantation of the artery. The scar tissue was interfering with the electrical impulses being sent through the heart, causing me to experience symptoms.

The doctor told me that I could have ablation done to destroy the tissue if necessary, but the first step would be to see if the symptoms could be controlled by medication. I started on heart medication right away and it worked miraculously! After experimenting with dosage for many months to find the right amount for me, I couldn't wait to finally try out some rigorous physical activity to see what my heart could do now that all of my problems were under control.

When I returned to speedwork in my running, I found that no matter how hard I pushed myself, I seemed to hit a wall that kept me from reaching speeds I easily held before my surgery. I trained harder, was consistent, and worked on strengthening my muscles, but nothing seemed to help me break through the barrier. It felt so good to have blood pulsing through my veins and to be running symptom-free again! I was deeply thankful for my life, my health and my return to training, but I couldn't understand why I was so much slower. I wondered if I would ever get fast enough to have the chance to finish my last two turns in Boston. That unfinished race, a small piece of the many joys stolen from the running community that dark April day, still called me to return and complete it but I wondered if my body had what it would take to get me back to Boston.

15

Courage to Try & Courage to Fly

In the three years after my open heart surgery, we adopted Isaiah, sent Kelsi off to college and had moved to a small town about 30 miles north of Camp Grace. I had run a few half marathons, completed a couple of triathlons and was back to training six days per week. Despite all of the hard work, I was drastically slower than I had been before my heart surgery. I wondered if I could even complete the full marathon distance again, let alone run it at a pace that would secure me a spot at the start of the Boston Marathon in Hopkinton.

My chance to give the distance a try came when Kelsi needed to raise money for a senior internship/mission trip to Paris. I racked my brain to come up with fundraiser ideas and the first to pop into my head was a run. I decided that the run had to have a bit of a crazy element to it to attract the sponsors we needed so I committed to running 53, half-mile laps around the parking lot of our local recreation department. Friends and family pledged to donate different dollar amounts for each lap I ran. We were amazed to see the donations add up to $1,300! As I completed each lap, supporters would add a popsicle stick to a small-scale, flat model of the Eiffel Tower I had constructed on a poster board. It took 53 sticks to complete the tower, so my run would be done when the tower was finished. We posted pictures of the progress of the tower on Facebook so donors could see the laps adding up. When the tower was complete, so was my first post-open heart surgery marathon.

I kept my pace at around 10:30 per mile since it was my first marathon in a long time and my goal was just to finish. My longest run leading up to the fundraiser was only 15 miles, but I found the 26.2 miles easy to finish because I kept such a comfortable pace. With God's provision and support from friends who came to run some laps with me and others who cheered me on from the sidelines, 53 laps were completed, securing the funds that Kelsi needed for her trip. More than that though, I was once again bit by the marathon bug.

I began looking at pace charts, calculating finish times, and looking up training plans to help me train for a qualifying marathon. Everything looked so doable on paper, but I had learned that the medicine I was on actually limited the heart's maximum rate during exercise. That wall that I kept feeling like I was running into was actually there, built by the medicine that was keeping my heart in rhythm. I was just so thankful that I could run that I felt guilty for wanting more. Wasn't being able to run enough for me? With all my scarred heart, I knew that I could be content no matter what my circumstances were. I knew what it was like to be immobile in a bed, the room spinning around me, and unable to care for my family. I would never forget what it felt like to fight for my life and wake up from emergency surgery, thankful just for the blood running through my veins. I knew that abundant life, for me, no longer depended on outside accomplishments but on living a life yielded to the One who gave me life.

Why then did I have a desire to run fast? Did being 100% content with what I had and wanting to see how much farther I could go have to be exclusive of one another? I was weeks into one of the training plans that I had settled on, try to get my speed up so I could be a contender to qualify. No matter how hard I worked, I couldn't reach my goal times in any of the distances and paces prescribed by my workout. The whole idea seemed pointless. If I was going to sacrifice my time, sleep and comfort to push for the goal, I wanted to see results. If they weren't guaranteed, because of the limits the medicine placed on my heart, then what was the point of trying? I lamented this dilemma while I was on the phone with my friend Brandy one day, telling her that I was going to quit the hard-core training and go back to be a runner thankful for each step forward. I was mostly sure that my heart couldn't rise to the challenge. "But you'll never know for sure if you don't try," she reminded me. She was right. I knew I could run, and I was overwhelmingly grateful for that, but I was only *mostly* sure that I couldn't run fast enough to run a Boston qualifier.

Mostly.

That word left room for some doubt. Just enough room for there to be a chance that I could overcome the limits placed by the medication and finish that race I had started years before- the race that terrorists stole from me. It was in that bit of space that I could run with gratefulness for what I had *and* push on to see if there was more that I could tap into. It was on the foundation of thankfulness that I would reach on to a higher goal. Like Brandy said, if I didn't even try to construct the dream, I would never know if it was even possible. The conversation between us two hard-nosed runners was the equivalent of the sweet and inspirational Peter-Pan-turned-nursery-decor quote: *"What if I fall?" "Oh, but darling, what if you fly?"*

I also had to reconcile within myself that if the sacrifice would be worth it if I did end up falling instead of flying. A committed marathon training program, for me, would start with a 12-week 5K training program to help me build speed. I would then move to a 10K or half-marathon program for another few months and then would finally start the actual 18-week marathon program. These programs would require at least 25 miles per week of running and at the most, just over 50 miles per week. The commitment I would be making would be nearly a year long and would add up to over 1500 miles, most of those being early morning miles that would cost me sleep and morning snuggles with my children. I would have to go to bed early on Friday nights because Saturday long runs would require an early wake-up call. I would run six days a week and with drive time in addition to my runs, would have to give up at least seven hours each week, almost equaling one full workday per week. I would have to get new running shoes a little more often because of all the miles accumulating on them and would have the expense of the registrations for actual races I would run to help me in my training. I would also have to give much attention to my diet, sacrificing comfort foods with foods that would fuel my training. I knew the cost of the goal and was willing to pay the price for a sure shot at a qualifying run. But was it worth the risk knowing that my chances were pretty slim? That answer would only come one year of hard training and two marathons later.

In the spring of 2018, after nine months of hard training, I ran a marathon and because of gastrointestinal distress that came on early in the race, I had a slow and disappointing finish. I gave myself a few weeks off and then jumped into a 5K training plan, followed by an 18-week marathon plan, with my sights set on running a qualifier in September of the same year, on the last possible weekend to qualify for the next year's Boston.

My sister, Amy, and I planned to run the marathon together in Erie, Pennsylvania. We followed the same training plan and, since we lived in different states, used an app to follow each other's training progress. While tremendously challenging, training "with" Amy brought me fulfillment and logging into the app to check on her daily runs became something I looked forward to each day. In group texts with her, our mom, and Amy's partner, Dani (who was also following the training plan with us), we shared our successes, struggles, menus and encouragement. I'm such a running geek and had spent so much of my training alone that, even though it was virtual, I loved every aspect of the support group we had formed.

Once again, Casey was 100% behind my effort to reach my goal, asking me about my training every day and even hanging around long enough to hear about it as I shared every detail of pace and distance. He helped me balance my training with our schedule and even rode his bike next to me on a couple of training runs.

My training took place over the summer, when my homeschooling responsibilities were non-existent, and my children enjoyed the summer pleasures of staying up late and sleeping in in the mornings. I was writing this book and training for the marathon at the same time. Six mornings per week, throughout the entire summer, I motivated myself out of bed with imaginary images of Amy and I crossing the finish line together in Erie under three hours and forty-five minutes and securing a spot in the 2019 Boston Marathon. When I got up early enough, I could run, go to the gym to work on my strength, and then write at a local coffee shop for an hour or two, all before the kids really got going in the morning.

Six weeks into the training plan, I quit my run halfway through one morning and came home with tears in my eyes. Casey immediately dropped what he was doing. "Why are you back so early and why are you about to cry?" he asked. "I just can't make my pace. I was supposed to run seven miles at my marathon race pace and I can't even make it three at that pace. If I can't even do that, how am I ever going to run 26.2 miles at that pace?" He waited before answering, knowing that I wasn't done. "You of all people know how hard I'm working at this but no matter how hard I try, I just can't break through this barrier! I'm not the same runner I used to be. Am I a fool for even trying, knowing that my heart medicine is working against me?" He waited for me to finish and then said, "I'm behind you whatever you decide but I don't think you'll be OK with yourself if you quit."

I shuffled through the day, weighing the same questions I had been struggling with off and on for some time. Every day, I went out for my runs with effort but when it got hard, I pulled back, reconciling that I needed to just be thankful that I could run. Somewhere in the middle of the ping-pong game of questions going back and forth in my mind, I realized that my medicine wasn't the only thing holding me back. I had spent four years living with such intentional gratitude for being alive, being active, and being able to run, that I was actually limiting myself with thankfulness. While I had learned that being thankful and striving for more at the same time was OK, I wasn't translating that knowledge into my actual running. Pulling back and falling back on gratitude became a cycle that actually kept me from mentally pushing my legs and lungs harder.

With my new understanding, I went out for a 10-miler the next day, ready with a different approach. When the effort got hard, instead of using thankfulness as a crutch, I leaned into the hard and pushed myself harder. I had to do this several times over the course of the run but doing so was creating a new habit in me. When the 10 miles was complete, I felt a sense of accomplishment that I hadn't experienced in a long time. I knew I had a breakthrough.

From there, I spent the next 12 weeks gaining speed and confidence. Once again, thankfulness was the foundation for my running, but I refused to stop there, knowing that a foundation was useless without something built upon it. Doubt in my ability to qualify became a stranger as I hit my paces day in and day out, feeling stronger with each passing day. By the time I landed in Erie to meet up with Amy, I was sure that I would fly out of there with the title of Boston Qualifier.

The night before the race, Amy and I went over our race strategy one last time. Our goal pace was 8:27 per mile. We agreed we would fight the temptation to go out too fast in the beginning. She had decided to train at my pace so we could run together. We also both agreed that while Plan A was for both of us to cross the finish line together in under 3:45, Plan B would be for at least one of us to run a qualifier. Over the months of training, Amy had become a stronger and more fit runner. With that and her ten extra minutes to qualify (she was in a different age group than me), I was confident she would make her goal and I was confident that I would do it too. However, we had to know how we would handle the situation if one of us were to fall off pace due to injury or exhaustion. We had both put so many hours and over 550 miles into our training. We had sacrificed so many comforts to get to that starting line that our love for each other kept us from wanting the other to be held back if one of us were to falter. I knew in my heart that if I couldn't run a qualifier, I would be just as excited if Amy could do it. She was there with me the year of the bombing and had to process her own grief after the attacks. If she had to make those last two turns on the streets of Boston in my place, it would be just as meaningful.

Race morning was marathon perfect. We both woke up feeling refreshed and prepared, the weather was cool, and the race would be pancake flat. Along with 2,200 other runners, we lined up on Presque Isle, PA and took off at the sound of the gun. After a slow first mile spent maneuvering through the crowded street, we settled into our pace and enjoyed the contented feeling that only hard work and preparation could have given us in that moment. The course consisted of two, 13.1-mile loops so we had to run through the start/finish line at the halfway point before we began our second loop. As we passed under the finish banner, completing our first loop, I began to fight back tears of joy, knowing that I was on pace and feeling as though I was sure to make my goal when we came back around to that point in just over 13 miles. Back at home, I had almost finished this book project so as the sound of the steps of hundreds of other runners who surrounded me tapped in my ears, I was writing this final chapter in my head, knowing that qualifying for the Boston Marathon would make a perfectly happy ending to my story. I had come so far and worked so hard and sacrificed so much. I would tell all who would read these pages that striving for your dreams is worth the effort! That even though when you reach for a goal you're not guaranteed to reach it, it's still good to go for it anyway. Because… what if you fly? As I ran on, I wondered if I should stop this story at the victorious and hard-won finish in Erie or wait six months to write the final chapter after I ran the last two turns in Boston.

I was jolted back to the present by Amy pulling a few feet in front of me. I was running a hard pace. Surely, I was on pace and she, excited by the race atmosphere, was going too fast. I reeled her in but when we clocked the next mile, I realized that we had slowed down and that her pace had been right on. She pulled me along through the next mile, trying in vain to keep me on pace. By mile 18, after several attempts to drop back and encourage me back onto pace, she guiltily stuck to our plan, keeping the pace and letting me fall back. She drifted out of sight as I enrolled every mental trick I had been practicing to help spur me on toward my goal. No matter how hard I tried, my body wouldn't rise to the challenge. My heart, limited in pumping capacity, struggled to push enough oxygen to my demanding muscles as fast as they required it. To compensate, my muscles leeched the oxygen carrying blood from my digestive tract, leaving me with an upset stomach in the slightest uptick in pace.

I had eight miles to watch my dream fade out of reach and eight miles to decide if the ride was worth the fall. Had it been worth it to give up all that I had to reach for a goal that I knew was mostly unattainable? Through those final miles, I had concluded that it was indeed worth every ounce of sweat and every step made. Courage isn't about doing the easy and predictable. In the easy and predictable, courage isn't even required at all. It took courage to commit to begin the hard work *without* the guarantee of success. It took courage to push on in my training when I didn't think I had the strength. And it took courage to see the training through to the end.

I embraced this new aspect of courage but most importantly, I embraced the lessons that grew from the effort that the courage had pushed me to give. I knew I was mentally and physically stronger because of my pursuit. I had identified and broken through barriers that I wouldn't have even known existed if I hadn't tried. I made myself get uncomfortable, get tough and demanded more of myself than I even knew I could give. And in the end, I had the opportunity to accept defeat, growing in ways that only perceived failure can teach. I firmly believe that failure is a greater teacher than success and I had become its student, desiring to once again soak in all that it had to instruct.

By the time I reached mile 25, it was all I could do to keep moving forward. I felt mentally strong, but my body had once again failed me. I became aware of the very real possibility that Amy, whom I hadn't seen for seven miles, had crossed the finish line and become a Boston qualifier. A smile spread across my flushed face as I pictured her striding under the banner that we had passed together just a dozen miles before with her hands raised over her head. Tears of joys streamed down my cheeks as I pictured her crying tears of joy, too. These thoughts carried me through the last grueling mile of the race. As I neared the finish line, Amy met me, as I pictured with tear stained cheeks, fighting the dual emotions of her accomplishment and my failure. She ran alongside of me, splitting away to let me cross the finish line of my tenth marathon and met me on the other side.

When I got back to our Airbnb after the race, I had dozens of texts from friends and family who were waiting to hear if I had qualified for Boston. Between my Back to Boston Facebook page and regular updates on Instagram, I had really opened myself up to exposure on my quest. Instead of sharing my victory story like I had hoped, my updates were the ones I fought so hard to avoid. On the surface, to everyone else I had failed.

However, I don't regret the year of training I poured into getting to that finish line, even though it was in a disappointing 3:57 instead of the triumphant 3:41 I had solidly aimed for. Like many others, my life has been a series of wins and losses and, while celebrating the wins came easily, I had to decide what to do with those losses. I had decided to make this one count as gain and that took courage that I knew came from the Lord. I never shed a tear over that failed attempt but instead gave thanks that I had been gifted by God with the grace to excitedly witness my sister take the path I was aiming for. He really can do exceedingly, abundantly beyond all we can think or imagine! Taken at face value, it looked like I had fallen but inside, with what the Lord was doing in my heart to help me process it, I felt like I was flying! It takes courage to fly when, to everyone else, it looks like you've fallen.

Epilogue

I was on aisle four of the Dollar Tree spending way too much time trying to decide on a cheap closet storage solution when I tuned into a conversation going on between two ladies who clearly knew each other, but obviously hadn't seen one other in a long time. The conversation jumped from generalities to specifics as one of the women asked how one of their mutual friends was doing. The other lady replied with shock, "Oh, didn't you know? She died a few months ago. It was her heart. She never had any problems but one day they found her in the shower... dead. They said she had an undetected heart problem."

"Oh no! I can't believe that. She was so young! And didn't she have a lot of children?"

"Yes, she had seven. And they're just lost without her."

I swallowed hard and fumbled with a stack of plastic baskets to seem as if I didn't hear. But tears welled up in my eyes as I struggled to catch my breath. I felt like I was getting to hear just one of the many conversations that would have taken place if my situation had gone differently. I had chills all over as the ladies carried on, bringing up so many similarities between their dearly departed friend and how my life could have ended. I couldn't escape the nagging question. It was even following me around the Dollar Tree: *Why didn't I become that story?*

After nearly being engulfed by the cords of death, why did I get to become Isaiah's mom? Why did God let me get to see my oldest child graduate from high school and then drop her off at college just a couple months later? Why did I get to be there to watch my children blow out more candles on their birthday cakes? Why did I get to add another year to my age? Why would the Lord allow me to experience another Mother's Day? Why did I get to run another mile? And then another? And then string 26.2 of them together three more times? Why did I have the privilege of pushing my body to its limits in training for those Boston qualifier attempts? Who was I to get more laughs, more memories and more joys?

For many months after my second heart surgery, I struggled with survivor's guilt, feeling like I owed something back for the extra chances I'd been given. In the months and years following my heart surgeries, I began to inwardly wrestle with these types of questions. I had to know why. Why God allowed me to live, despite slow paced medical treatment/response and why he allowed me to have symptoms for nine years from a condition that usually shows up first with sudden death. I also wondered why I was the daughter who got to be Kitty- not just the crazy-little-cat-girl-Kitty but the Kitty with nine lives who, by age 37, had already used so many of them. What was I supposed to do with that?

I also needed to know *how* I could know for sure that I was living my life with a purpose that would really matter. In some ways, I felt like I had the added responsibility of making mine a life worth saving. I wondered how I needed to change my life to make sure that each day was counting for something that mattered. How was I supposed to show that I was thankful to be living on borrowed time?

Besides finishing Boston, I had so many ideas: I wanted to wear red every day in the month of February for Women's Heart Health Awareness Month. I would host a 5K in February, too, right near my birthday in honor of a life saved and all the funds would go to the American Heart Association. I could wear a purple ribbon for Chiari awareness and join a support group for Chiari sufferers. My heart also felt happy when I thought about starting a ministry that goes to hospitals and nursing homes and provides physical touch to the patients. No gloves performing medical tests, just a skin-to-skin hand to hold. Casey's attention to this detail for me propelled my recoveries greatly. I also had a desire to campaign to get others active and taking care of the one body they have for life. In the weeks of heart surgery recovery, I contemplated everything from starting a speaking ministry to becoming a doctor. The chances I'd been given left me pressured to do something, anything, to make it count.

My life has had a lot of little lives dependent upon it and though I wanted to give to others who were facing what I have faced, my days filled up so fast with meals to make, laundry to do, lessons to teach and bedtime stories to read. So out of all the great, others-focused, life-impacting ideas I had, I didn't do any of them. Not. Even. One. But I finally got to the point where I was OK with that. I learned that making this life count didn't mean I had to start a charity, fulfill a bucket list, or become a spokesperson.

Everywhere I go, people are amazed and shocked at my life story because it's already so unusual. They ask questions, drop jaws and beg to know more. God wrote this story and I share it whenever I can. I hope that counts. But I finally found comfort in knowing that this saved life doesn't have to be a big bang just because it holds life-changing scars. It doesn't have to impact like a tidal wave. It can be a slow and peaceful moving stream that unassumingly changes the landscape while bringing refreshment to the few that meet up with it. More specifically, my life can have significance and can be worth all the saving, all the lives, if it just means that I've been given the extra time to care for my family. If they can be the ones refreshed, watered, growing and cared for, then my life will still have mattered.

Practically, this means that I don't cross off my bucket list, post it to Facebook and get the glory all while my children are left holding empty buckets in my absence. It means that being there to read to them at night and, after my morning runs, greeting them with a cheerful good morning song, is worth being alive for. The day-to-day mundane tasks of washing their dishes, teaching them letters and leaving them sticky notes matter.

On the sixth month anniversary of my closest brush with death, I let my mind drift to what life would be like if I hadn't pulled through that horrific ordeal. Six months would have passed since my husband would have had to be strong for the kids while he watched a box holding my broken body get covered in dirt. There would have been 526 meals that they would have had to prepare without my help. Most impactfully, those meals would have been eaten with an empty space at the table. Close to 600 loads of laundry would have had to have been washed, dried, folded, and put away. 728 hours of homeschooling. Seven children with five subjects each. Why only seven? Because we couldn't have welcomed Isaiah to our family if I wasn't there to care for him. 182 days of my husband waking up in an empty bed, having to figure out how to face another day of raising our large family alone.

In all this calculating, I have learned that courage can be quiet and subtle. Courage can be turning down good and rewarding opportunities in our lives that can distract us from our most important focus. Practically this means saying no to the good so we can say yes to the better. Being there for the normal and mundane, I learned through this, takes a greater amount of courage than is required for showing up for the big and bold. While I didn't immediately create something from my tragedies that others could rally behind and praise, the Lord has given me the courage to show up every day and give my best to the ones who need it most. It was those who need me the most- my children- who helped me learn my most recent, and most impactful, lesson in courage.

With brain surgery, a bombing, two heart surgeries and a string of other trials in my life, I have at times felt like I had my share of hardships and that life should be smooth sailing from now on. Anyone who has lived a while on this orb knows what an unrealistic expectation that is. Yet, after so many years of being thrust into learning the ins and outs of courage, I somehow believed that I had served my time. However, while focused on simply being mom and wife, a whole new level of courage was exposed to me.

Earlier this year, one of my children faced a situation that tore them apart. As a mom, it was heart wrenching to see my child suffer emotionally. But as I prayed about it, asking the Lord to fix the problem, I felt the direction of my prayers changing. In a change of heart that I couldn't take credit for, I began to thank the Lord for allowing the difficulty in my child's life. I felt like the Lord gave me a glimpse into what the other side of the situation was going to look like and what I saw was that, whether or not things worked out the way we wanted them to, my child would be closer to the Lord because of the loss.

Another one of my children suffers from anxiety and depression. We have walked a long and difficult road with this one and are still in the midst of the struggle. She recently joked about how much easier my life would be if she were normal and teased that she was my hardest child. She seemed to inwardly conclude that I would be happier and better off if she wasn't here. As I contemplated her comments and the years of struggle I've had with her, I realized that I couldn't agree with her. Yes, my life would have been *easier* if she didn't face deep emotional struggles. I won't lie. Even so, I see her as a wonderful gift. Without her and her individual needs, I would have fallen back onto my old way of thinking that I had it all together and wanting other people to come to the same conclusion. Pride would have overtaken me as people stood in awe of our large family who "had it all together." I have actually grown to appreciate that her struggles make it impossible for us to hide behind a curtain of perfection that could have easily fallen back into place. Because of her, I grew from hoping no one would notice our problems, to being thankful that people saw the real and the hard. I hoped that others would see that we weren't pushing through on our own strength but that the Lord was walking us through... one helpless, yet courageous, step at a time. I also found myself able to relate to others who were dealing with hard parenting issues without me looking down on them, thinking they were only having problems with their kids because of their own shortcomings as parents. I knew I only had this perspective because of the challenges I've faced and was repulsed at the thought of who I would have been without it. I couldn't welcome the result without welcoming the trial that lead me to it. I knew that the struggles had the same effect on my daughter and found that her beauty radiated through her scars, making us both stronger.

Building on this realization, I began to see a trial coming, as if it were a rain cloud forming in the distance and learned to thank the Lord as the storm hit for how it would strip, water, and ultimately strengthen us. Courage isn't limited to asking for help *in* the storm or giving thanks for the lesson *after* the rains have stopped. Courage slowly grew to living as it says in the Bible in the book of James, considering it... "pure joy whenever you face trials of many kinds because you know that the testing of your faith develops perseverance and perseverance must finish its work so that we may be mature and complete, not lacking anything."

The hardships that I had endured taught me lessons that could only have come from facing those storms. I knew that while I wouldn't have chosen the difficulties, I was forever changed by what they taught me. I learned to lean into the Source of courage and discovered his strength was there for me every step of the way. I was challenged to turn from fear and to embrace courage. I began to understand that God gave us just the courage and strength we needed for whatever was immediately facing us. I discovered that courage is sometimes facing a difficulty head-on and at other times is putting situations out of our minds until it's time to deal with them. I knew that it took courage to grieve, courage to try and courage to fail. Above all, I was sure that I didn't possess an ounce of courage on my own but, through letting go of myself and my expectations, could press into the One who is an everlasting source of it.

The fabric of my life was woven from these lessons and, though it was tattered and scarred, they made my garment strong, vibrant, and beautiful. Sharing this weaving process was the very reason that I chose to finally write this book. But as I was sitting down, hour after hour, to give words to my story, the Lord was writing this final chapter in my own life and answering this all important question: If courage is to be desired and trials are the only way to get it, then why had I sought to avoid them instead of quietly thanking him when I saw one coming over the horizon?

When I was training for a recent marathon, I valued fast times over the strength difficult terrain would give me in the long run. I found myself seeking any flat land I could find so that I could clock my best times, giving myself a sense of accomplishment. It's our human nature to want the fast and easy to avoid the difficult at all costs. This idea of having the courage to welcome hardships was almost incomprehensible to me. But as the Lord began to expose this new level of courage, I aimed to avoid the flat roads that only gave me a false sense of my own strength. Instead, I head for the hills, the steep inclines and demanding terrain that I know will grow and shape me to be more like the One who made me. The Lord gives the courage to fight up the hill. He gives the rest at the peak. He is also the one who fills us with the courage to thank him for the hill as we approach it. This idea is beautiful to picture but it's even more beautiful to see a life living a courage that welcomes the hard.

Sometimes courage comes just one step at a time but sometimes courage can fill us with gratitude before we even have to lace up our shoes to climb the mountainous road ahead.

Made in the USA
Columbia, SC
05 July 2024

SILVER WATER COLLOIDAL

SILVER FOR HUMANS' HEALTH, WELLNESS, AND HEALING

WAYNE ROWLAND
With Herb Roi Richards

waynerowland.com

Terms and Conditions

LEGAL NOTICE

The Publisher has strived to be as accurate and complete as possible in the creation of this work, notwithstanding the fact that he does not warrant or represent at any time that the contents within are accurate due to the rapidly changing nature of the Internet.

While all attempts have been made to verify the information provided in this publication, the Publisher assumes no responsibility for errors, omissions, or contrary interpretation of the subject matter within. Any perceived slights of specific persons, peoples, or organizations are unintentional.

In practical advice books, like anything else in life, there are no guarantees made. Readers are cautioned to rely on their judgment about their individual circumstances and to act accordingly.

This book is not intended for use as a source of legal, business, therapeutic, accounting or financial advice. All readers are advised to seek services of competent professionals in legal, business, therapy, accounting and finance fields.

ISBN: 9798883476579